UNUSUAL RAILWAYS

UNUSUAL RAILWAYS

by

JOHN R. DAY, A.M.Inst.T.

and

B. G. WILSON

FREDERICK MULLER LTD.
LONDON

FIRST PUBLISHED BY FREDERICK MULLER LTD. IN 1957
PRINTED IN GREAT BRITAIN BY EBENEZER BAYLIS AND SON, LTD.
THE TRINITY PRESS, WORCESTER, AND LONDON
BOUND BY THE DORSTEL PRESS LTD., HARLOW

CONTENTS

ILLUSTRATIONS

ILLUSTRATIONS

ACKNOWLEDGEMENTS

The authors' grateful acknowledgements are due to the following for information and general assistance:

J. Brockhouse & Co. Ltd.; E. Evan Davies, Esq., Managing Director, Snowdon Mountain Railway; General Post Office (Public Relations Department); Walter Keller, Esq.; T. S. Lascelles, Esq.; D. C. Lawrence, Esq., Librarian & Curator, Dick Institute, Kilmarnock; Charles E. Lee, Esq.; Monorails Inc.; New Zealand Railways; Puiseux, Durin & Cie.; Régie Autonome des Transports Parisiens; United States Information Service; H. A. Vallance, Esq.; W. Yorath Lewis, Esq.

For the loan of photographs or drawings, or permission to reproduce them:—

Bridgnorth Castle Hill Railway

Curator of Historical Relics, British Transport Commission

General Post Office (Public Relations Dept.)

Glasgow Corporation Transport Dept.

Kent & Sussex Courier

R. F. Legget, Esq.

Librairie Hachette, Paris

Modern Transport

Puiseux, Durin & Cie.

New Zealand Railways

ACKNOWLEDGEMENTS

New Zealand Tourist Office, London

Public Relations & Publicity Officer, Western Region, British Railways

Régie Autonome des Transports Parisiens

W. G. F. Roberts, Esq.

Winston Robinson, Esq., General Manager & Engineer, Brighton Corporation Transport Dept.

C. E. R. Simpson, Esq.

The Smithsonian Institution, U.S.A.

Swiss National Tourist Office

Wuppertaler Schwebebahn

Mayor J. Walker, of Jim Thorpe (formerly Mauch Chunk), Pa., U.S.A.

AUTHORS' NOTE

The many systems described have been chosen for their general interest. They range in time from ancient Greece to the present day and are numerous in type, even though in a book of this size we cannot claim to be exhaustive. Where one system combines two or more principles it has not always been easy to decide in which chapter to include it, but we hope that our decision has been logical. Where possible, contemporary accounts have been drawn on.

CHAPTER ONE

SHIP RAILWAYS

THE idea of carrying ships overland goes back to the earliest times. The movement of vessels as large as 150 ft. in length and 18 ft. in beam from the Aegean to the Ionian Sea across the Isthmus of Corinth was recorded in 427 B.C. and it was believed then that the method had been used for many years. It was effected by a ship railway probably composed of parallel stone blocks, into which grooves were cut, and which the Greeks called *diolkos*. The traffic made Corinth one of the foremost maritime cities of the Peloponnesus. The "railway" was abandoned with the decline of the commercial supremacy of Greece, after an existence of at least 400 years.

It is not recorded that the Romans moved ships overland by such means, and the next application of the principle seems to have been by the Venetians in A.D. 1438, when 30 galleys were hauled from the Adige to Lake Garda by 1,000 oxen, aided by windlasses on the steeper inclines. Fifteen years later there took place the most spectacular application of the method, one which helped considerably to change the course of civilisation. When he laid siege to Constantinople in 1453, Soleiman Pasha, who had apparently heard of the Venetian exploit, avoided the chain stretched across the Hellespont to stop him by moving his fleet in a single night over greased timber ways, laid on trestles, into the Golden Horn, beneath the walls of the city.

In 1718, Emmanuel Swedenborg, then a humble

engineer, was raised to the nobility for successfully conveying vessels overland from Stromstedt to Idelfal, in Sweden. The first large-scale adoption of overland ship transport in Britain came in 1826, when boats on the Bude Canal were moved up and down seven inclined planes. Small iron wheels on the boats ran on two lines of rails, and the boats were lifted by an endless chain, worked by two tanks alternately filled with water and descending into wells.

A remarkable system of railways, portage railways, and canals was developed in Pennsylvania in the 1830s, making it possible to travel by the system from Philadelphia to Pittsburgh. One of the most distinguished travellers by this route was Charles Dickens, who described it in his *American Notes*.

The route comprised four distinct sections, all owned by the State of Pennsylvania. Passengers and goods were put at Philadelphia into half a canal boat, which was then pulled on a trolley by horses through the streets to the terminus of the Philadelphia & Columbia Railroad. There the sections of the boats were placed on railway wagons, hauled originally by horses but later by locomotives, as far as Columbia. At Columbia the boats were assembled and entered a canal for the next stage of the journey to Hollidaysburg at the foot of the Alleghanies. Once more they were dismantled and placed on rail as before. The third stage was over the Allegheny Portage Railroad through the mountains to Johnstown, where the boats were put together a second time to complete their journey by another canal to Pittsburgh.

The Allegheny Portage Railroad included ten rope-worked inclined planes, linked by level sections worked by locomotives. The line was $36\frac{1}{2}$ miles long, laid with rolled iron edge rails in cast-iron chairs resting on stone blocks. Two 35 h.p. stationary engines provided the power on each incline. The planes varied in steepness from $7\frac{1}{4}$ to $10\frac{1}{4}$ ft. in 100 ft. They were later replaced by an adhesion-worked deviation line. Not long after being taken over by the Pennsylvania Railroad the whole of the Portage Railroad was abandoned in favour of the P.RR's own main line, which included the celebrated horseshoe curve near Altoona. The Philadelphia & Columbia also had two inclined planes, with rope haulage, at its termini. In the 1830s a similar portage was brought into use on the Morris & Essex Canal in New Jersey.

Sir James Brunlees proposed in 1860 to Napoleon III that a ship railway should be built to carry vessels at 20 m.p.h. across the Isthmus of Suez. Although he estimated that it would cost only one-seventh as much as a canal, de Lesseps, to whom the proposal was referred, gave preference to his own canal plan. No greater success attended a later plan for a ship railway to avoid the Nile cataracts.

Although the success of the Suez Canal might have seemed to be a blow for the advocates of the ship railway, they were undaunted, and claimed that their system was far cheaper and easier when difficult country had to be traversed. At one time a Captain Eads proposed a ship railway across the Isthmus of Tehuantepec in southern Mexico and gained from the Mexican Government a concession allowing him to build a line on any route he selected, on condition that work began within 2 years from the date of the agreement and was completed within 12 years. He was to have a right-of-way half a mile wide, with an extra half mile for stations. The length was 112 miles and the estimated cost was $75,000,000. The United States Government was to have the option of lending aid. It was considered a healthier route than one across the Isthmus of Panama and more direct for

American ships. The Mexican Government was empowered to take possession of the works after 99 years.

At Minatitlan, some 25 miles from Gulf of Mexico, in the deep River Coatzacoalcos, a basin was to be excavated to admit vessels to the lifting dock, about 450 ft. long and 75 ft. wide and 12 to 15 ft. deep, formed of steel plates with stout bulkheads, and able to raise vessels of 6,000 to 7,000 tons. The roadbed was to be about 50 ft. wide, with rails of 100 to 120 lb. per yd. resting on steel sleepers 50 ft. long, supported on 2 ft. of stone ballast. The only gradient was to be 1 in 100 for 12 miles. Baldwins proposed to supply three locomotives of a type built for the Dom Pedro Railway, Brazil, which would be able to haul vessels of the largest size envisaged at 15 m.p.h. up 1 in 132. Floating pontoons would allow vessels to pass, or a change of direction to be made. Although Eads's scheme was supported by British naval experts nothing came of it. At length the Atlantic and Pacific were linked by the Panama Canal.

In 1889, William Smith, Harbour Engineer of Aberdeen, explained in a lecture to the London Chamber of Commerce the advantages of his flexible ship railway over the rigid type proposed by Eads. Both systems, said Smith, used the principle of distributing weight over many wheels, but his provided also for the uniform distribution of the pressure of the load over the hull of the ship, changes of direction by railway curves instead of cumbersome pontoons or turntables, and changes of level by railway gradients. Smith proposed to use hydraulic cushions, sectional cars with adjustable sides, and compound bogies. The last-mentioned were two trains of carrying trucks on each of the seven lines. The railway would end in a slipway at both ends.

Although the Tehuantepec line did not materialise, the professional endorsement which it received helped to gain the passage of an Act to build a ship railway across the Isthmus of Chignecto in Nova Scotia, a narrow neck of land between the Gulf of the St. Lawrence and the Bay of Fundy, to save vessels at least 500 miles. For years, schemes for a canal had been mooted, but had been defeated by cost and the heavy maintenance involved in view of the range of tides in the Bay.

The idea originated with one H. G. C. Ketchum before Eads's scheme. An Act authorising the Canadian Government to subsidise the project was passed in 1882 and amended in 1886 when the Chignecto Marine Transport Railway Co. Ltd. was incorporated. The roadbed was to consist of two parallel tracks 18 ft. between centres and laid to the standard gauge. The rails were to be of Vignoles type, 110 lb. to the yard. The line was to be dead straight, 17 miles long, with a maximum gradient of 1 in 500. The cradles to carry the vessels were to be formed on double transverse girders mounted on bogies. The ship would be blocked in first along the keel, and secondly by wedge blocks secured under the bilge. Vessels of up to 1,000 tons could be handled. Motive power was to be eight-coupled tank locomotives, built by the Canadian Locomotive & Engine Company. Two locomotives abreast were to haul each vessel. Sir John Fowler and Benjamin Baker were the engineers, with Ketchum, and John G. Meiggs & Son the contractors (Meiggs was a brother of Henry Meiggs, the engineer of the Peruvian Central and Peruvian Southern Railways).

Vessels were to enter a large basin 500 ft. long and 300 ft. wide, with a lifting dock at the inner end. There, hydraulic presses would raise them 40 ft. on a supporting gridiron and cradle. At the top the vessel and cradle, resting on wheels, would be moved hydraulically to the railway. The time estimated to raise, transport, and lower vessels was estimated at 2 hours. Work began in 1888, but a financial crash in which they were involved caused the contractors to suspend it in 1891. Fresh financial arrangements were made and another firm, S. Pearson & Son, of Westminster, was entrusted with the completion of the work. The Canadian Government agreed to allow an extension of time, provided that the company guaranteed a certain amount of traffic before claiming the subsidy of $170,000, which it had originally promised on completion of the line. Even so, new difficulties arose and the scheme languished and died. Only a few relics of this project are to be seen today.

A similar but more ambitious scheme for a ship railway to link directly Lakes Ontario and Huron was put forward in 1892. A company, the Ontario Ship Railway, was incorporated to build a three-track railway to convey lake vessels between Toronto and Collingwood, 66 miles. This was no more successful.

The use of locomotives on the banks to haul vessels along canals seems to have originated with Hyde Clarke, an engineer who in a letter to *The Railway Magazine* in 1838 said that he had put forward the idea in 1836 but the ironmasters had decried it, fearing that the greater speed would create a ruinous wash. For existing canal banks, Clarke proposed—because of the narrowness—a single rail only and a narrow locomotive with six wheels, two running on the rail.

In August 1839 a trial of locomotive haulage took place on part of the Forth & Clyde Canal. The locomotive, *Victoria*, ran on a single track laid on blocks and was attached to each passenger boat which came along. It reached a speed of over 17 m.p.h. Subsequently, the experiment was successfully repeated with masted vessels and cargo boats.

The most impressive example today of the mechanical towing of vessels by railborne vehicles is on the Panama Canal, where ships are moved through the locks by electric locomotives called "mules".

Four of these locomotives are required to tow a vessel of moderate size, two ahead (one on each wall) and two trailing behind to keep the vessel in the middle of the locks and bring it to a stop when entirely within the lock chamber. Each locomotive consists of a body and two bogies, the body containing a motor-driven windlass for hauling in or paying out the towline under load and a high-speed motor-driven attachment for coiling the line when it is out of service. The windlass drum incorporates a friction device to prevent the load on the tow line exceeding 25,000 lb. The body is supported by a partly-flexible connection at each end on a bogie. The two bogies are identical, containing traction motors and control apparatus.

When towing or taking the 1 in 2 inclines between the lock, the locomotive operates as a rack-rail tractor, being propelled by the traction motors driving the rack pinions through gearing. These rack pinions are of quill construction type and mounted on the back axle of the bogie, allowing the bogie wheels to run free. The towing speed is 2 m.p.h.

In returning, except on the inclines between the lock levels, the locomotive travels under friction tractive effort at about 5 m.p.h.; this change of speed is provided for by throwing in jaw clutches connecting the wheels of the bogie with the traction motors. The motors have brakes which can stop them in fifteen revolutions when running at full speed. The railway on which the locomotives travel is of 5 ft. gauge.

The traction motors have a full-speed torque of 840 lb.

at 1 ft. radius and a full-load speed of not less than 470 r.p.m., and are able to develop at least 75 per cent greater torque for a period of 1 minute. The motor for the windlass has a full-speed torque of 120 lb. at 1 ft. radius and a full-load speed of 660 r.p.m., and can exert 50 per cent greater torque for 1 minute. The motor for coiling the cable is smaller. All of them are 3-phase, 25-cycle, induction motors of the railway or mill type. Current is taken from a conduit containing two conductors, the third phase being carried by the track rails.

When the approaching vessel is made fast fore and aft to towing locomotives on each side, it is centred by means of adjustment of the cables on the locomotive. The apparatus is so fixed in the locomotive that the cable will then slip or pay out only if the pull exceeds 25,000 lb. With a sufficient number of locomotives on each side this possibility is minimised.

CHAPTER TWO

RACK AND SIMILAR SYSTEMS

THE idea that a locomotive with smooth wheels could haul trains over a smooth track was regarded with grave suspicion in the early days of railways. The horses used for motive power got a good grip from the ground between the rails, but no locomotive could do this. How then could the locomotive work? Some form of positive grip, it was thought, was needed.

With this in mind, John Blenkinsop, in 1811, patented a system using a pinion on the locomotive which engaged teeth at the side of the rails. Blenkinsop was probably well aware that the locomotive could move along quite happily without the rack, but he felt that a light locomotive, lacking adhesion weight, could haul a much heavier load if it had a positive grip. Increasing the adhesion weight beyond a limited amount was impossible on the lightly-built lines of the day.

A locomotive on this system is said, in 1829, to have hauled a 140-ton train up a slope of 1 in 440 at some 3 m.p.h. The Blenkinsop system was installed on the Middleton, Kenton, and Coxlodge colliery lines in 1812–13. The Leeds–Middleton Colliery line is particularly interesting as having been, at least partly, operated by rope traction—possibly wholly so. Its conversion made it probably the first steam railway in Britain. An 1825 account of the line, which was sanctioned in 1758, makes it clear that there were two levels linked by an inclined plane some 350 yd. in length, at a slope of 1 in 24. The account says: "The first level is about two miles in length, one half of which is embanked from four to 12 ft. in height; the other level extends to the colliery, being about a mile in length, half of which consists of heavy embankment. On each of these, a locomotive engine, attended by a man and a boy, propels 26 loaded wagons, carrying upwards of two tons each, at the rate of four m.p.h.

"A brake is placed at the summit of it, which carries up four empty wagons by the descent of four loaded ones. *A* is a horizontal wheel, 16 ft. in dia., the rim of which is made of wood, about 9 in. broad, with a groove in it to receive the rope, and the lower edge hooped with iron. *B* is a flexible rim, made of several thicknesses of lath, lined or hooped on the inside with iron; this rim surrounds the rope wheel, and is suspended by chains just so as to clear it. It is made to collapse on the rope wheel by the lever *C*, so as to check the velocity of the loaded wagons at any time during their descent, and ultimately to stop them at the head and foot of the inclined plane, by the pressure of the suspended rim against the revolving rope wheel. The roller over which the ropes pass, on the gallows *F*, should be so placed as to be in the line of the plane continued. The time required for the transit of the set of wagons over the brake is less than a minute; it is attended by one man . . ." [Unfortunately, we are unable to reproduce the print to which the letters refer.]

Steam traction came in on 12 August 1812, the track having been laid with Blenkinsop rails. The line was worked by the Matthew Murray locomotives *Salamanca*, *Prince Regent*, *Lord Wellington*, and *Marquis Wellington*. The rack rail survived until 1835.

In 1825, the year of the account quoted, America's first railway locomotive was being built by Colonel John Stevens of Hoboken, New Jersey. It was interesting as combining the principle of guide wheels—for the four wheels had no flanges and were kept to the track by rollers hung at the lower ends of vertical bars and running against the inside surfaces of the rails—and rack and pinion drive. There was a water-tube boiler with 20 tubes, which can still be seen at the United States'National Museum, and a pressure of 550 lb. p.s.i. could be sustained. It stood upright on the locomotive. Wood was dropped to the circular grate through a door in the conical hood which covered the top of the boiler. The steam, taken from a pipe in the top header, drove a single-cylinder engine geared to a pinion which, in turn, engaged a rack between the rails.

The locomotive was intended for demonstrations only, but the small circular track for it, laid down on the lawn of Colonel Stevens's garden at Hoboken, was America's first steam railway.

In passing—for it was never used—mention must be made of an ingenious form of rack invented by a Mr. Snowden in Britain. In 1824 he took out a patent for a system which employed two flat-topped rails. On them ran a car fitted with broad flangeless wheels. On the centre-line of the car was a vertical rod fitted with a capstan above the deck of the car and with a large horizontal pinion at rail level. The teeth of the pinion engaged with the teeth of a rack rail laid on its side, with the teeth projecting horizontally, beside one of the rails. The car was kept on the track by horizontal guide rollers mounted in the same vertical plane as the pinion and running in a sort of trough rail laid in the centre of the running rails. When the broad running wheels veered too much from the centre of the rail surfaces the rollers engaged with one side or other of the trough.

The car was driven by manual labour turning the capstan. In a pamphlet published in 1834 it was suggested that this work would supply "ample employment . . . for all industrious labourers throughout the country." Perhaps no man wanted to be a galley slave, for no more was heard of Mr. Snowden.

A combined adhesion and rack locomotive, the first locomotive to be so fitted, came on the scene in the 1830s. It was built by the Neath Abbey Iron Works for the Dowlais Ironworks. Most of the detail drawings, which are dated from September 1831, to March 1832, suggest that the locomotive was to have been named *Success*, but someone has crossed out the name on one of the drawings and written in "Called the *Perseverance*".

A contemporary account of the feats of this locomotive appeared in the *Cambrian Quarterly Magazine* for 1833. It said: "The *Perseverance* engine, got up by the Neath Abbey Iron Company, South Wales, and supplied with the assistance of a rack running parallel with the tramplates from Penydarren to the Dowlais works, has accomplished the amazing task of conveying from the Dowlais Works to the basin of Cardiff Canal, $126\frac{1}{4}$ tons of iron at once, besides the weight of engine, tender, and wagons $50\frac{3}{4}$ tons, making an aggregate of 177 tons. The engine, after waiting several hours for the discharge of the iron, returned to the works with her complement of empty wagons, and ascended the side of the mountain, by means of the rack, with ease, without stopping for steam. The fact is the more remarkable from the road winding in some places excessively—and for the first nine miles of the road from the basin having an ascent of from $1\frac{3}{4}$ to $7\frac{1}{4}$ in. in a chain, and the last two miles $25\frac{1}{2}$ to $48\frac{1}{8}$ in. per chain."

A drawing reproduced in *Engineering* in 1867 shows a locomotive built in 1836 with similar characteristics to *Perseverance* and also built by the Neath Abbey works. It represents a six-coupled locomotive driven by inclined cylinders. As with so many of the early locomotives, there was a great deal of gearing, and the final drive to the trailing axle was through gearing from a shaft tucked under the rear end of the boiler. This shaft was itself driven by cranks from the connecting rod. The driving shaft also worked the valve gear—again through gears, cranks, and a shaft, and was geared to another shaft carrying the pinion which could be engaged with the rack at will.

That the Neath Abbey works had an inventive designer on the staff is shown by a small locomotive built by them in 1840, in which an attempt to improve adhesion was made by providing a large driven roller which ran between the rails on the track foundation.

In the U.S.A., an experimental rack and pinion line was built in 1847 between Indianapolis and Madison, and in 1848 two special Baldwin-built locomotives went into service on it. These had outside cylinders driving eight coupled wheels. An unusual feature was the provision of a separate pair of cylinders to drive the pinion. As with the Neath Abbey locomotives, the pinion could be disengaged from the track at will, a steam cylinder supplying power for the purpose. This line seems to have been short-lived.

The next important step in the development of the rack railway was also taken in America where in 1852 Sylvester Marsh, of Chicago, is said to have lost his way in bad weather on Mount Washington. He and a friend were compelled to spend the night in the open, an experience he never forgot. Marsh retired a few years later and he worked on the idea of a railway which could carry people comfortably to the top of the mountain to enjoy the view that he himself climbed the mountain to see. From the summit of the 6,293-ft. peak, the highest in New England, it is possible to see for 100 miles on a clear day.

By 1858, Marsh had progressed to the stage when he had built a model locomotive and could apply for a

charter allowing him to build railways to the top not
only of Mount Washington, but also Mount Lafayette.
His model was eyed with curiosity and met with some
derision from the New Hampshire Legislature, but he
got his charter. The next step was to raise funds, which
proved difficult, though some were raised by showing
the model locomotive in Marsh's Boston office, where
it regularly pushed a load of 50 lb.—three times its
own weight—up a 20-ft. track.

Tiring of trying to gain funds, Marsh decided to
build a section of track and a locomotive at his own
expense, and on 29 August 1866, he gave a demonstration of his railway on Cold Spring Hill, on the
slopes of Mount Washington. This aroused some
enthusiasm at last, and a company was formed with
Marsh as President. Work on the main track started
in May 1867, and had been completed to the foot of
"Jacob's Ladder" by 1868. This section was opened
on 14 August of that year, but work was pressed on
and by July of the following year the railway was open
to the summit, where the hotel built in 1852 formed a
natural upper terminus. No great fuss seems to have
attended the opening day, but a few days later President Grant made the trip to the upper station and
the seal of celebrity was placed on the line.

The original locomotive, *Old Peppersass*, which
weighed 8 tons, worked the line for 12 years before
being replaced. After a number of exhibition appear-
ances, it was taken into the care of the Baltimore
& Ohio Railroad. In 1929 it was hauled out, restored,
and returned to the Mount Washington Cog Railway.
The peculiar name is derived from the resemblance its
vertical boiler and wide chimney gave it to the pepper-
sauce bottles of the day. After its return in 1929 it
actually ran in steam up the mountain, but broke a
cogwheel on the way down and ran away. The driver

told everyone on the locomotive to jump off as contact with the rack had been lost and the handbrakes could not be applied quickly enough. A photographer left his jump too late and was killed as he fell.

The line today is very much as it was first built, with an average gradient of 1 in 4 steepening to 1 in 2½ on Jacob's Ladder. Seven steam locomotives are in use, named *Mount Washington, Ammonoosuc, Base Station, Summit, Great Gulf, Tip Top,* and *Waumbek. Old Peppersass* stands, though not on the main track, at the Base station. The locomotives have two pairs of cylinders, each pair driving on to its own pinion, and the passenger coaches also have pinions for control purposes and can be braked independently of the locomotive by a brakesman on the car. As is usual with rack railways, the locomotive pushes the coach before it and descends in front of it. Locomotive and coach are not coupled. The distance is 3¼ miles and the ascent takes 70 minutes.

Before leaving this line, mention must be made of a method of riding down the track employed by track maintenance men and long since banned. Wood and metal seats some 3 ft. × 1 ft. were made to fit over the rack rail. These were known as slide-boards, or more popularly, as "Devil's Shingles". Seated on these, controlling (sometimes) the speed with hand brakes, the men would career down the mountainside. The record time for the trip—as we have said, 3¼ miles— was 2¾ minutes! After one man had been killed and another seriously injured, the Devil's Shingles were banned.

During this time things were stirring in Switzerland, often regarded as the home of rack railways, but, as indicated, by no means their birthplace. It is said, though without reliable evidence, that Sylvester Marsh was invited to Switzerland to build a rack railway up

the Rigi. He would not go, but is reported to have
shown his models and plans freely to the Swiss engineers who went to America to see him.

A Swiss engineer named Wetli, however, produced
a system of his own in 1868. This was tried out on a
line from Wädensweil to Einsiedeln, a well-known
centre of pilgrimage. The line was about 10 miles
long. Each "tooth" of the rack was represented by
two straight pieces of rail inclined at 25 deg. to the
axis of the railway and meeting in the middle to form a
"V". The legs of each "V" overlapped the point of the
one behind it so that the series of "Vs" was continuous.
The legs were carried almost to the running rails. The
pinion which engaged these giant teeth was a roller with
projecting ribs so shaped that they would, if laid flat,
have fitted closely outside each "V" of the track. The
design was, in fact, a double helix.

If the cylinder were placed in position on the line
with the extremities of one of the ribs overlapping and
in contact with the extremities of one of the "Vs", and
then revolved, the ribs would wind themselves up the
slope (the points of the "Vs" faced up the slope) until
the point of the ribbing reached the point of the "V".
By that time the extremities of the ribs would be overlapping the extremities of the next "V", making the
grip continuous.

Rods were provided to link the wheels of the locomotive with the ribbed cylinder. A four-coupled tank
locomotive was used on a line built by a company
formed by Wetli in 1871. Some 10 km. of the line was
to have been on the Wetli system with gradients of as
much as 1 in 20, but Wetli ran into financial difficulties.
However, a 408 km. length of line on 1 in 20 was
opened in 1874, and the success of the trials held on it
was such that the line was completed. Further trials
were carried out in October 1876, with one of the

four-wheel locomotives built by Esslingen.   It was
found that the ribbed roller tended to rise out of the
"Vs" and then fall back into contact again and damage
the track.

Trials were resumed on 30 November after the
damage had been made good. The locomotive and a
wagon reached the top but trouble with the roller
developed again almost at once when the descent began.
It was therefore decided to retract the roller, which
could be done at will, and descend by adhesion only.
Unfortunately the train got of control very quickly.
Four people were on the locomotive and ten, including
directors and engineers, on the wagon. Most of those
on the wagon jumped, one being killed in so doing. As
the descent continued at increasing speed the coupling
between the locomotive and wagon broke and the
wagon was then brought to a stand, those who had
remained in it being saved. The locomotive ran on at
high speed and overturned and was wrecked at the
lower terminus, killing one of the three men still on it
and injuring the other two seriously. This accident
discredited the Wetli system, though it was not in use
at the time of the accident, and the line was altered to
work by adhesion only.

The study of rack railways had also been going on in
Italy, where a Signor T. Agudio invented a system in
which an endless motor rope replaced boiler and
cylinders as the source of motive power. Power from
the rope was communicated through a "locomotor"
to a pinion gearing into a fixed rack.

The Agudio system was first used in 1862 on a steep
slope at Dusino on the Turin & Alessandria Railway.
It was found to work at half the cost of conventional
locomotives. The French Government was interested
in this and in 1868 it ordered large-scale trials. Work
was started at Lanslebourg in Savoy and the line

was opened in 1874. It was single-track and worked
by a single "locomotor". The endless rope was in the
centre of the line with the two spans, up and down,
lying side by side. At the top and bottom of the incline,
the rope passed round a horizontal driving pulley
driven by a steam engine.

The ascending rope passed first round an auxiliary
pulley, next round the "motor pulley", and then continued up the slope. A pinion or friction wheel on
the motor pulley shaft worked the towing-wheel, or
adhesion pulley. This pulley wound itself up the slope
along a separate steel rope, secured at the top of the
incline and provided with a straining apparatus at the
bottom of the slope.

The Dusino incline was 1.4 miles in length, 1 in 37,
and included a 382-yd. curve. The Lanslebourg incline
was rather less than a mile in length, with an average
gradient of 1 in 3.82. The "adhesion rope" was replaced
by a central rack made of flat steel bar, $4\frac{3}{8}$ in. $\times$ $\frac{1}{2}$ in.,
which had been corrugated to roughly the same section
as an ordinary rack. This was laid on edge, thus pre-
senting a corrugated face to each side. Shallow
channel-irons were bolted to the top and bottom of the
corrugated bar, and the whole assembly was mounted
by bolts on a longitudinal sleeper.

The motor rope was used as before, but only the
ascending portion was used for traction. In fact, two
ropes were used, one on each side of the line. Power
was supplied to the rope by two turbines, each 6 ft. in
diameter, mounted near the foot of the slope, and
geared to the horizontal driving pulleys.

The "locomotor" consisted in essence of two large
grooved pulleys round which the motor rope passed.
These were connected by gearing to two pinions mesh-
ing into the rack. The inventor claimed that almost
twice as much traffic could be handled by his system as

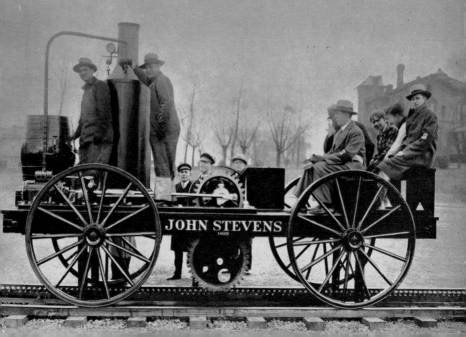

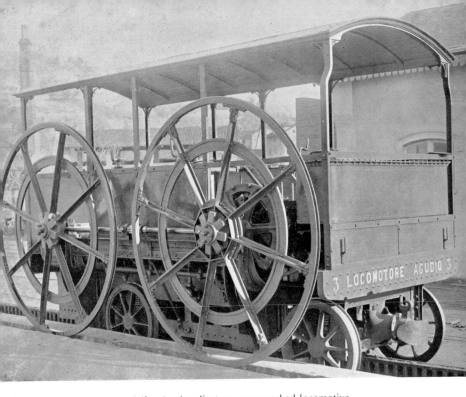

(*Above*) Agudio-type rope-worked locomotive.

(*Below*) "Old Peppersass" on its stand at the Base Station of the Mount Washington Cog Railway, with "Ammonoosuc" about to take a train to the summit.

(*Photo: R. F. Legget*)

by locomotives, with only a third of the outlay. Water could be used, through turbines, as the driving force, higher speeds could be attained, and steeper slopes could be surmounted. It is not at all clear, however what advantage was gained by using the "locomotor", as it would seem that the same turbines could have been used to wind a traction rope attached to the train as with an ordinary funicular.

In 1863, Nicholas Riggenbach, Locomotive Superintendent of the Central Swiss Railway, patented an idea for a rack railway and locomotive. He had made no application of this method when the news of the line being built by Marsh in the U.S.A. came to his hearing. He went to America to see this system and found that he and Marsh had had, quite independently, very much the same idea.

On his return he built an experimental line in some quarries near Berne. This worked well and two engineers, Messrs. Naeff and Zschokke, were particularly interested in the rack principle invented by Riggenbach. They joined forces with him and obtained the concession for the construction of a rack railway up the Rigi, which had recently been in the news as the result of the description published by Heinrich Keller, a geographer, of the fine views from the summit.

The concession for the line up the 5,905-ft. mountain was obtained from the Canton of Lucerne, a point which was later to have important repercussions. Work on the line was pressed forward and in May 1871, the new rack line was at Staffelhohe, less than 700 ft. below the summit but more than a mile away from it. The lower terminus was by the lake, at Vitznau. At Staffelhohe the boundary of the Canton of Lucerne was reached and the neighbouring Canton of Schwyz, on whose territory the rest of the line would have to be built, would not give permission for the line to continue, for it was considering a railway of its own. Eventually the Canton of Schwyz laid its own line from Arth-Goldau, on the other side of the mountain, but it relented to the extent of building the section from the summit to Staffelhohe first and allowing the original line running powers over it in consideration of a rental. The line was thus completed in June 1873, the Canton Schwyz line following two years later.

Riggenbach's line was 4·38 miles in length with a maximum gradient of 1 in 5. It included the 240-ft. Schwanden Tunnel and the 235-ft. Schnurtobel Bridge. The rack system was an improvement on that used on the Mount Washington line. It was laid centrally between the rails of the 4 ft. 8½ in. track and consisted of two channel irons 4¾ in. deep and 2⅜ in. wide with a half-inch vertical web. The channel irons were 5 in. apart and the wrought iron teeth of the rack itself were riveted into the channel irons at both ends. Tapered teeth were used, locking the pinion into the rack and resisting any tendency for the pinion to climb out of it, a principle which has been used in most rack systems ever since. Wooden sleepers were used at first but were replaced by iron ten years later when the line was relaid with steel rails.

The first locomotive, like that of Marsh's line, had a vertical boiler mounted on a four-wheel frame. Outside cylinders drove an intermediate shaft on which were mounted two pinions which, in turn, drove the driving axle, the front one, by gearing. The driving axle also carried the pinion which geared with the rack. The rear axle, on which the wheels ran loose, carried also a spur wheel which engaged the rack. This locomotive pushed up the incline a coach carrying 54 passengers. This was not coupled to the locomotive and was fitted with efficient brakes of its own.

For normal braking on the descent, a system of

reversing the valves admitting steam to the cylinders was used. Air was drawn into the cylinders, compressed by the movement of the train, and this gave braking resistance. Later locomotives had outside cylinders also but a larger driving pinion was used which had to be placed on a separate axle behind the leading wheels. A centrifugal governor, afterwards compulsory on all Swiss rack lines, controlled the speed automatically. A special rack brake worked on the rear axles.

The Riggenbach principle was used on both the Rigi lines, which are now electrically worked, and also on a line from Rorschach, on Lake Constance, to Heiden, also now electrified. Several lines in South America used the Riggenbach rack, including the Leopoldina line, where it was used for a mountain section rising to the resort of Petropolis. Here the line rises 842 metres in 6 km. with a maximum gradient of 19 per cent. It was also used for the Corcovado Railway, Rio de Janeiro, a metre-gauge line from the Largo do Carioca to the top of Corcovado Mountain. This line climbs 2,300 ft. in just over two miles. It was opened, with steam locomotives, on 1 July 1885. The steepest gradient is 1 in 3·3. Steam traction continued until 1910 when the line was electrified on the three-phase system. It is of interest that Riggenbach rack locomotives were built by Baldwin, in America, for the Estrade de Ferro Principe do Grao Para, Brazil, and an illustration of such a locomotive appears in *The Railway Engineer* for October 1889.

Another Riggenbach line was constructed in 1874 up the Kahlenberg, near Vienna. The line and its locomotives resembled closely those already described, and readers living near London can see a model at the Science Museum at South Kensington representing the wheels and motion of one of the locomotives, and also, of course, the rack itself. This particular railway included a gradient of 1 in 10. Two Swiss electric railways on the Riggenbach system are the Schynige Platte line, near Interlaken, and the Wengernalp line. An unexpected place to find the Riggenbach rack was in Angola, in Portuguese West Africa, where a rack portion was incorporated to overcome a 1 in 16 gradient on a 2-km. section between Lengue and Sao Pedro. An avoiding line enabled the use of this section to be discontinued in 1948.

We now come to a system which was not a rack-and-pinion method at all, but bears so many similarities otherwise that this chapter is the natural place for it. This was the Fell system, which used a central rail against which auxiliary wheels were pressed to gain extra adhesion. It is doubtful whether Fell was the originator of the system, though he may have thought of it independently, for a similar invention by Ericsson and Vignoles appeared in 1830. Later patents were filed by Teller in the U.S.A. and Kraus in Hanover. It is claimed in France that Séguier originated the system and that others who worked on it were Dumery, Giraud, and Fedit.

As far as we can discover, the first patent was taken out on 30 September 1830, by Charles B. Vignoles, the British engineer, and John Ericsson, the Swedish engineer. On 15 October 1840, a patent was taken out by Henry Pinkus, described as "an English gentleman", whom we meet elsewhere in this book. On 18 December 1843 Baron Séguier wrote to the Paris Academy of Arts & Sciences, proposing the use of a centre rail to prevent high-speed trains leaving the lines—not as a means of climbing gradients, it will be noted. On 5 December 1846 the Baron took out a patent describing himself as the inventor. Yet another patent was taken out by A. V. Newton in England on 13 July 1847. The first patent by John Barraclough Fell was taken out on 20 January 1863 and on 16 December of the same year, under the description of "improvements in locomotive engines and railway carriages", Fell took out a second patent. He did not claim that he had invented the centre rail, but only the particular means of applying it.

Fell instituted experiments between 1863 and 1865 on the Cromford & High Peak Railway, in Derbyshire, where an 800-yd. length of line, of 3 ft. 7½ in. gauge, was laid out on the Fell principle. The section is stated to have included 180 yd. of straight track with a gradient of 1 in 13 and 150 yd. of 1 in 12, with curves of 2⅜ chains each. The centre rail was raised 7½ in. above the surface of the running rails. The principle of the Fell system was that horizontal wheels beneath the locomotive were pressed by an arrangement of springs and levers against the sides of the centre rail. The horizontal wheels were driven and added their power and grip to those of the adhesion wheels. The effect of this extra grip became clear in the course of the trials.

The trial locomotive had two horizontal wheels and had 12 in. dia. cylinders of 18 in. stroke. The boiler pressure was 120 lb. p.s.i. The four coupled wheels were of 2 ft. 3 in. dia. The weight of the locomotive, complete with water and coke, was 16 tons. It proved capable of taking a load of 24 tons up the slope, and as much as 30 tons in good conditions. When the horizontal wheels were taken out of use, the best load the locomotive could manage was 7 tons.

These experiments were so satisfactory that, for the benefit of the French Government, it was decided to hold large scale trials on the slopes of Mont Cenis. The condition was laid down that if the experiments should prove successful, a concession should be granted of part of the roadway for a Fell line to be laid across the French portion of the mountain on similar terms to those already agreed for an Italian portion by the Italian Government.

The trial line was about 1¼ miles long and ran from a point 5,305 ft. above sea level at Lanslebourg to 5,820 ft. The gauge was the same as that on the High Peak section—3 ft. 7½ in.—and the gradients were similar, with an average of 1 in 13 and a maximum of 1 in 12. Commissioners representing England, France, Italy, Austria, and Russia were in attendance at the trials, which lasted some three months in the spring of 1865. Strangely enough, it was found that the rails offered better adhesion when swept clear of the snow than in summer when the line was clear. This was because, once swept clear, the rails were perfectly dry in the cold weather, whereas in summer, dust and moisture made them slightly slippery.

The locomotive employed in the High Peak trials was taken to Mont Cenis, but most of the trials there were made with a locomotive built specially for the line. It had an unladen weight of 13 tons, which was increased to 17 tons 2 cwt. with coke and water on board. There were two cylinders of 15-in. dia. and 16-in. stroke which acted on four normal driving wheels and four horizontal wheels at the same time. The boiler pressure was 120 lb. p.s.i.

With three wagons, weighing about 16 tons, this engine climbed the incline at 11 m.p.h. against the 7½ m.p.h. which had been promised the French Government. The horizontal wheels could each exert a pressure of 2½ tons on the centre rail, or 10 tons in all, but this could be controlled by the driver from the footplate so that less pressure could be exerted on suitable sections of the line and unnecessary friction avoided. It was found that in all 48 tons could be handled on the slope. In his report to the Board of Trade, Captain Tyler, who held a watching brief for the British Government, said:

"Few would, in the first instance, either contemplate or witness experiments on such steep gradients and round such sharp curves on the mountainside, without a feeling that much extra risk must be incurred and that

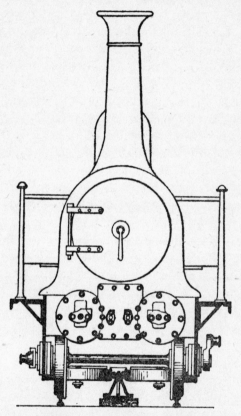

FIG. 1. Fell locomotive for the Mt. Cenis railway, showing the centre rail and horizontal wheels

the consequences of a fractured coupling or a broken tyre, or of a vehicle leaving the rails, would on such a line be considerably aggravated.

"But there is an element of safety in this system of locomotive working which no other railway possesses.

"The middle rail not only enables the engine to surmount, and to draw its train up these gradients, but also affords a means of applying any required amount of extra brake power for checking the speed, or for stopping any detached vehicles during the descent, and it further acts by the use of horizontal guiding wheels on the different vehicles as a most perfect safeguard, to prevent engines, carriages or wagons from leaving the rails. . . . The safest portions of the proposed railway ought indeed, under proper management, to be those on which, the gradients being steeper than 1 in 25, the middle rail will be employed."

The Emperor Napoleon III was said to have taken a warm interest in the experiments and to have intervened personally in the matter of granting the portion of road taken for the railway. As a result of the trials, as Sir Cusack P. Roney stated in his *Rambles on Railways* (1868)—a neglected book from which many of the facts about the early days of the Fell system have been taken—a decree was issued on 4 November 1865. It stated that Napoleon III authorised the construction and working of a locomotive line between St. Michel and the frontier of Italy—the summit of the pass— until "the opening of the tunnel of the Alps" for traffic.

Work started on 1 May 1866, but floods caused much damage in September of that year. The trial trip on the completed line took place on 26 August 1867. The line was laid at the outer edge of the existing roadway for the most part, but it crossed the road 33 times, of which 17 crossings were on the level. Wooden sleepers, 3 ft. apart, were used. The centre rail was laid on longitudinal timbers fastened to the sleepers and stood 9 in. above the running rails. There was an arrangement whereby this raised rail could be lowered into a recess at level crossings by pulling over a lever.

A description of the Fell system by a contemporary of Fell's, Mr. J. M. Heppel, a civil engineer, said:

"The vertical and horizontal wheels of Mr. Fell's engine are all driven from one pair of cylinders, and so coupled that they must all revolve exactly together; so that, abstracting for a moment from the slip or scrub of the vertical wheels which takes place on curves, if one slips they must all slip; and so long as the total adhesion is sufficient to take up the power, it is a matter of very little importance how it is distributed among them.

"The adhesion of the vertical wheels is due to the weight of the engine, and for any given condition of the rails, is a constant quantity. On the other hand, the adhesion of the horizontal wheels is, within its maximum limit, completely under control, and is given by a powerful screw motion, acting upon springs, which keep them always pressed against the rail with a force practically uniform. Notwithstanding any small inequalities of dimensions, all therefore that is requisite in ascending a heavy incline, is to set up the screws till the adhesion of the horizontal wheels makes up with that of the vertical ones, the total amount required for utilising the traction power of the engine."

A French journalist describing the opening of this line must have had Swiss influence very much in mind, for he wrote that "the railway is laid on the system of the distinguished Swiss engineer, M. Guillaume (William) Tell"!

On the other side of the mountain the line ran down to Susa, and the through journey of 48 miles took 7 hours 9 minutes, including station stops. It was operated for some $3\frac{1}{2}$ years, during which 100,000 passengers were carried without serious accident. After the opening of the Mont Cenis tunnel the line was closed, as had been the original intention, and the Fell rails were shipped to Brazil to be laid on the Canta-Gallo Railway, a 20-mile coffee line.

When the railways of the North Island of New Zealand were being built it was necessary, at a point some 34 miles out of Wellington, to take the Wairarapa railway through the Rimutaka Mountains. To have followed a route with reasonable gradients would have been very costly, and steep gradients had to be accepted. Cable haulage with winding engines was considered but the route curved so much that the idea was abandoned as impracticable and the Fell system was chosen.

The line climbed almost 1,000 ft. in the 14 miles from Upper Hutt to Summit. There were long gradients of 1 in 35 and numerous sharp curves. Although every advantage was taken of the lie of the country it was necessary to build three short tunnels, and there were also three tunnels on the eastern side, where the line dropped 869 ft. in three miles. As against the average of £11,400 per mile for the line from Wellington to Featherston, including all equipment, the Rimutaka incline cost over £29,000 a mile. Even then it was estimated that the acceptance of gradients of 1 in 15 reduced costs by more than £100,000.

Four 0-4-2 locomotives of Fell type were designed by H. W. Widmark, a Swedish engineer, and built by the Avonside Engine Company, of Bristol, in 1875. Two additional locomotives to the same design were built in 1886 by Neilson & Company, of Glasgow. These locomotives worked all traffic on the incline for some time and were supplemented by ordinary adhesion locomotives in the early part of this century. The Fell locomotives could each handle 65 tons on the 1 in 15 stretches. Trains of up to 260 tons were allowed, the locomotives being spaced out along the train so that each had its proper load. Speeds were not high, being limited to 6 m.p.h. going up and 10 m.p.h. on the descent. To control the train on the way down, special Fell brake vans were added to the trains. A 250-ton train needed five of these vans, each with a trained guard in charge of the brakes, which bore on the centre rail. The sight of a full train, with its series of locomotives, fighting its way up the incline will not be seen again, for on 3 November 1955 a 5-mile tunnel was opened which takes the line through the Rimutakas. The Fell line is no longer used, but one of the locomotives is being preserved.

The Fell system is used on one line in the British Isles, the Snaefell Mountain line in the Isle of Man, a branch of the Manx Electric Railway. This line is built on the 3 ft. 6 in. gauge and is worked by bogie tram-type vehicles. In point of fact, the Fell apparatus is not necessary for the ascent, and is used only for braking on the way down. Snaefell, the "Snow Mountain", rises to 2,034 ft.

There was a period of revival of interest in the Fell system in the year or two after the first world war, and a patent was taken out by G. Nobel Fell for centre-rail locomotives. In January 1919 *The Railway Engineer* carried an article by G. Nobel Fell in which he proposed either electric locomotives or locomotives driven by "gaseous fuel". Drawings of the electric locomotive showed two six-wheel bogies. The centre rail also acted as a conductor rail. The horizontal wheels were to adhere by magnetism to the centre rail and electro-magnets would also apply centre-rail brakes. The internal-combustion locomotive would have been either petrol-electric or coal-gas-electric and have been of 4-4-0 wheel arrangement. It was claimed that a modern centre-rail system, with electric traction, would make possible mountain railways with gradients of 1 in 15 or 1 in 10.

Before leaving the Fell system we must mention a strange little line built at Aldershot in the early 1880s on a system which had something in common with the Fell principle. This system used two longitudinal sleepers of wood or iron supported by posts and strutted for transverse stability. Rails of 10 to 18 in. gauge rested on the longitudinals. The rolling stock was balanced by small horizontal wheels on each side which bore against the sides of the longitudinals some 7 to 13 in. below the rail surface, the actual distance being proportionate to the gauge of the track, The carriages were extended below the track level on each side and passengers sat back to back sideways to the track. An experimental line with a gauge of 8 in. was laid down for about a mile near Barrow-in-Furness, probably in 1870. The Aldershot line was 1880 yd. in length and extended from Aldershot to South Camp (Signal Hill). It included a 250 yd. viaduct and a gradient of 1 in 50.

It was built of timber, each sleeper consisting of three planks laid on edge and bolted together, supported on piles. The rails were of Vignoles pattern and the gauge 17 in. On the outside of the sleepers were fixed two square bars of hardwood to take the pressure of the horizontal wheels. The cars on this line were actually suspended from the axles, so that there were similarities to the Lartigue system described in another chapter. The cylinders of the locomotive were below rail level and were connected to cranks on the central axle, the leading and trailing wheels being coupled to the centre wheels. The wheels themselves were inside the frames and the cranks and cylinders outside.

As the horizontal wheels also guided the train, flanges were not needed on the running wheels. Passenger trains are said to have run at 20 m.p.h. and

30 m.p.h. to have been attained in safety. This system was proposed for a line between Lausanne and Ouchy, where a funicular was eventually built instead. The French took an interest in the system and its use was considered for carrying army supplies in the Franco-Prussian war, but the war ended before anything was done.

In passing, it may be mentioned that in 1872 the Chief Engineer of the Downpatrick, Dundrum & Newcastle Railway, in Ireland, one William Lewis, is said to have proposed a rack railway from the resort of Newcastle, Co. Down, to the summit of Slieve Donard, some 2,800 ft. above sea level. Lewis had considerable correspondence with Sylvester Marsh in America on his rack system. Though reconsidered by the Belfast & County Down Railway early this century as a tourist attraction, the line has never materialised.

Another type of rack widely used in Switzerland was patented by Dr. Roman Abt in 1882. In his system teeth are cut in the edge of a metal bar, which is then turned on edge and secured between the normal rails. A second metal bar, cut like the first, is secured beside it so that the teeth of one bar are opposite the gaps in the other. The locomotives are fitted with a double pinion, also stepped to engage with the stepped track. This gives smoother running and continuous firm engagement.

The system was designed at the instance of Albert Schneider, who had been entrusted with building a line into the Harz Mountains. He consulted Abt, who for many years had been associated with Riggenbach. This line was built at Blankenberg in 1884. At the time of the 25th anniversary of the system it was calculated that 55 lines used the Abt system. Of these, seven were in South America, one in Australia, one in Japan, two in India, one in the U.S.A., many in

Switzerland, and one in Wales. In all, there were 317 Abt locomotives.

The first electrically-operated rack railway, on the slopes of Mont Salève in France, close to the Swiss Canton of Geneva, was built in 1890-93 on the Abt system. It used a gauge of one metre and was 5½ miles in length. Current distribution was by third rail on porcelain insulators outside the track, and this is thought to have been the first line in Europe on which this type of distribution was used. The maximum gradient was 1 in 4. This rack line has since been replaced by a cableway.

The Abt line in the U.S.A. is of great interest because of the great height to which the line is carried. The summit of Pike's Peak is 14,147 ft. above sea level and affords views over an area of 60,000 sq. miles. Work on the line began in 1884, but after the roadbed had been carried to 6,629 ft. above sea level and was eight miles from Manitou technical criticisms caused the work to be abandoned.

When the success of some of the Swiss rack railways had been demonstrated work began again. Instead of the 30 miles of the original plan, with maximum gradients of 1 in 20, the new line was to be only nine miles in length, but with gradients as steep as 1 in 4. The surveyors began work, under very difficult conditions, in 1888. Their work was hampered by deep snow for half the year, but eventually they reported that the line could be built but the hazards of thick snow must be met.

In 1889 work began on the easier lower slopes. All construction work was in steel or stone and the track was laid on heavy ballast. Through the forested lower slopes the work was easy, but above the tree-line solid rock was met which had to be blasted away. In other places ledges had to be cut in rock faces. The cold, the rarefied air, and the strong winds took their toll of the energy of the builders, but on 20 October 1890 the last rail of the 47,992-ft. line was laid.

On 1 June 1891, four-cylinder Vauclain compound locomotives took the first trains, with their Pullman type coaches, up the mountain. The line had cost £22,000 a mile and the last few miles were through hard-packed snow and ice. The Vauclain compounds have gone out of service now and diesel locomotives take the trains smoothly upwards, but perhaps some of the romance of this high mountain line has gone with them.

The company has seven steam, one petrol, and three diesel-electric locomotives. The steam locomotives are now used only when the line is very busy. Many characteristics are common to all the locomotives. The tractive effort comes entirely from the pinions engaged with the rack rail. The outside wheels are only for carrying the load. The locomotive is always below the coach and pushes it up the mountain and precedes it on the way down. It is not coupled. If an accident should happen to the locomotive it does not affect the coach, which has its own independent braking system. In more than 60 years of operation, there has never been an accident.

The last two diesel locomotives placed in service have two diesel engines with a maximum power of 275 h.p. at sea level. At the altitude of Manitou, the power falls to 225 h.p. and it goes down to 190 h.p. at the summit of Pike's Peak. The maximum speed is some $12\frac{1}{2}$ m.p.h. on most of the route and half that on the steepest sections. The line is operated from 1 June to mid-October each year, weather conditions permitting. The timetable shows two ascents and descents a day, but extra trains are run as required.

The one and only rack railway in Britain, the Snowdon Mountain Railway, is laid on the Abt system. It starts from Llanberis, some 350 ft. above sea level, and climbs at gradients ranging between 1 in 20 and 1 in 5·5 until it reaches the upper terminus, slightly below the actual summit of the mountain, which is 3,560 ft. high. The total rise of the railway from terminus to terminus is 3,140 ft. and its length is 4 miles 54 chains. The average gradient is 1 in 7·83. The rack is used for the whole length of the line, and on all sidings and turnouts, as well as in the engine and carriage sheds. The line is single, but three passing places or turnouts are provided at roughly equal distances, as well as a double track at each terminal station of sufficient length to hold a full train. The sharpest curve is of 4 chains radius.

The crossings on the Snowdon Railway are of a complicated design, as the rack is carried right through, making a continuous track for the engine pinions. The switches are 12 ft. in length, the radius of curve being 151 ft. $3\frac{3}{4}$ in., the rate of crossing about 1 in $4\frac{1}{3}$, and the angle 13 deg. The rods and levers which work the points are connected with and work hinged portions of the rack which are brought into the correct position at the same time as the points are thrown over. This provides the continuous rack for the pinions of the engine, and also clears a passage for the bearing rails. No crossing is placed on a steeper gradient than 1 in 10.

The locomotives were built by the Swiss Locomotive & Machine Works, Winterthur, Switzerland. Nos. 2-5 weigh 13 tons $5\frac{1}{2}$ cwt. when empty, and 17 tons $5\frac{1}{2}$ cwt. when in running order with full load of coal and water. They are guaranteed to be capable of taking a load of 18 tons up a gradient of 1 in $5\frac{1}{2}$ at a speed of 6·7 km.p.h. The indicated horsepower is 166. The cylinders are of $11\frac{13}{16}$ in. dia., placed outside the frame, and the stroke is $23\frac{5}{8}$ in. The motion is communicated

The Vitznau-Rigi Railway in its early days, showing original "coffeepot" type of steam locomotive.

Present-day Vitznau-Rigi train.

(Photos: courtesy of Swiss National Tourist Office)

(*Photo: High Commissioner for New Zealand*)

(*Above*) A train descending the 1 in 15 gradient of the Rimutaka incline, worked on the Fell centre-rail system and now superseded by an adhesion line, less steeply graded and including a five-mile tunnel.

(*Below*) Snowdon Mountain Railway trains crossing halfway up the mountain.

(*Photo: H. D. Keilor*)

to the cranks by a one-sided rocking lever with upper and lower connecting rods, and the fulcrum of the rocking lever is kept as low as possible. The valve chests are above the cylinders. There are three axles, the leading and second each having pinion wheels attached, and being coupled together, while the third is on a trailing pony truck.

The wheels are carried inside the frames, and are all loose on the axles except one of those on the trailing axle, which is keyed. The first and second axles have solid forged discs in their centres; to each of these discs are attached two steel pinion rings, so set that their teeth alternate. There are 15 teeth to each pinion ring. In order to hold these pinion rings in their relative positions on the axle discs, and at the same time to allow slight circumferential movement to prevent jarring, and also to allow for any slight irregularity in the pitch of the teeth of the rack bars, eight double horseshoe springs are inserted in the disc under each pinion ring. The upper ends of the springs project into countersunk spaces on the inner or under side of the rings. The maximum play allowed is 3 mm. To avoid more play being obtained in the event of one of these springs snapping or becoming weak, a solid iron tongue is introduced. The springs and pinion rings are held in position by the brake drums, being placed on each side, and being firmly bolted through the solid forged axle discs with eight steel bolts $1\frac{1}{8}$ in. in diameter.

This description refers to the original locomotives supplied for the opening of the line—now reduced to Nos. 2-5. No. 6 was added in 1922 and Nos. 7 and 8 in 1923. They resemble the earlier locomotives in most particulars but are superheated and are a little heavier, No. 6 weighing 18 tons 8 cwt. in working order and the other 19 tons 13 cwt. All are named.

Locomotive No. 1 had a very short life. On the opening day of the line, two trains climbed the mountain. No. 1, *Lidas*, took the second. On the way down, *Lidas* left the rail and dived into a ravine. The boiler was torn off and the engine landed upside down. She was completely wrecked. The train of two coaches behind her stayed on the track and was held by the hand brakes. The driver and fireman jumped and were saved, but a passenger in the train leaped out and was killed. The line was then closed. The cause of the accident was presumed to have been the buckling of the rack by frost, causing the pinions to ride up off the track.

For greater safety in future guard rails were laid down beside the track and grippers fitted to the locomotives. The grippers pass underneath the guard rails, making serious derailment virtually impossible. The line opened for traffic again in April 1897.

The first six bogie coaches were built by the Lancaster Carriage & Wagon Company to Swiss designs. They had seven compartments for eight passengers each, and a special compartment for the guard. They were 38 ft. over buffers, 6 ft. 6 in. wide, and 9 ft. 4 in. high. The coaches had canvas curtains for wet weather, and, like the locomotives, were fitted with grippers for the guard rail. There were also a few wagons. Some of the coaches have now been rebuilt with improved bodies. Another coach came from Switzerland in 1921 and two more in 1922. All hauled, or rather pushed, rolling stock has a pinion which engages the track and is used for friction braking.

The 91-mile Beirut–Damascus Railway has a 19·8-mile Abt rack section with gradients of up to 1 in 14. All its rack locomotives were built by the Swiss Locomotive & Machine Works. The first series, of 0-6-2 type, can haul 85 tons on the rack sections and the powerful second series of ten-coupled locomotives can haul 140-ton goods trains up the slopes.

Carrying the story back to Switzerland, mention must be made of the exceptionally steep rack railway which runs from Alpnachstad, on the shores of Lake Lucerne, up Mount Pilatus. This line, built between 1886 and 1888, was so steep that no rack then invented would have been safe enough for the purpose. The line climbs 5,344 ft. in 2¾ miles and has an average gradient steeper than 1 in 3 and sections of 1 in 2. Dr. E. Locher, the engineer of the line, devised a special system for this railway. This has a flat rack rail in the centre of the track, laid horizontally with teeth cut in both its sides. The pinion wheels of the original steam cars and the present 'electric cars are mounted horizontally in pairs and engage each side of the rack rail. The car is thus not only propelled but also automatically centred on the track. This feature has enabled flanges on the carrying wheels, which run on ordinary rails, to be dispensed with, thus making it easier to round the many sharp curves of the line. This line is so steep that the coaches themselves are arranged in a series of steps so that the floor in each compartment is kept more or less horizontal. The approach to the summit is particularly thrilling, as much of it is on a ledge cut in the face of a sheer precipice. A special feature of the line is the use of traversing points, ordinary points being regarded as unsafe on so steep a grade.

The rack railways of Switzerland form a fascinating study in themselves, but space does not allow us to describe others in detail. Of particular interest is the Furka–Oberalp Railway, which has a bridge over a gorge that becomes an avalanche track in winter. After early bridges over this, the Steffenbach Gorge, had been swept away each winter, a collapsible bridge was designed which is now folded up before every winter and unfolded again in the spring. There are no winter trains, of course. There is also the group of railways which leads to the summit of the Jungfrau and the highest railway terminus in Europe, at 11,333 ft. The last 3,470 yards took six winters to build, all in a tunnel in the mountain, with the upper terminus, Jungfraujoch, just below the actual peak of the Jungfrau, and also in the tunnel. The tunnellers suffered greatly from cold and the rarefied air. Its next highest rival is the Gornergrat Railway, which reaches 10,235 ft. above sea level and is entirely in the open air. There is also the Brienzer Rothorn line, opened in 1892, which, now that the Monte Generoso line has been turned over to diesel operation, is the last steam-operated mountain line in Switzerland.

Last of all, a mention should be made of J. Hanscotte, Chief Engineer of the Compagnie de Fives-Lille, whose work on the Fell system is too often forgotten. His main improvement was the rearrangement of the frame carrying the horizontal wheels so that it had a certain mobility within the main frame of the locomotive, and also the use of compressed air instead of springs to press the wheels against the Fell rail. When a railway linking the Rhone valley with the Rhine valley over the Furka and Oberalp passes was proposed the Hanscotte system was suggested— it had already been used for the railway from Clermont-Ferrand to the summit of the Puy-de-Dôme in France. The Swiss Locomotive & Machine Works designed a locomotive, but at the same time constructed, for comparison, an Abt locomotive. The latter proved superior and led to the adoption of the Abt system.

CHAPTER THREE

CABLE-WORKED RAILWAYS

AS it was not at first thought practicable for locomotives to surmount very steep gradients without
aid, recourse was had to endless rope haulage, a practice which originated with mines and spread naturally
to mine railways.

On the Canterbury & Whitstable Railway, opened on
3 May 1830—the first passenger railway in the south-
east of England—trains were hauled by rope for
four miles out of Canterbury and by locomotive for
the remaining two to Whitstable. The first stationary
engine was at the top of the Tyler Hill incline and
pulled the trains up from the Canterbury terminus. At
Tyler Hill the rope was detached and that controlled by
the next engine house, Clowes Wood, was attached.
From Clowes Wood coaches ran down by gravity to
the point where the locomotive was attached; they
were followed after an interval by the wagons of the
train, let down by a rope which was then available for
hauling trains up.

The steepest gradient was 1 in 28 on the descent from
Clowes Wood towards Whitstable. The engines at Tyler
Hill and Clowes Wood each developed 25 h.p.; there
was also a 15 h.p. engine at South Street, near Whitstable. The rope was $3\frac{1}{4}$ in. in circumference.

A stationary engine at Swannington, Leicestershire,
installed in 1833 to the designs of George Stephenson,
the engineer to the Leicester & Swannington Railway,
and supplied by the Horsley (Coal & Iron) Company,
West Bromwich, is exhibited at the Railway Museum

in York. It is exceeded in age only by that at Middleton, Derbyshire, referred to later. Originally the main flow of traffic was loaded coal wagons up the incline ($\frac{1}{2}$ mile at 1 in 17). Now the only loads are downhill. The coupling of the leading wagon of empties is connected to the rope by a slip coupling. At the top the slip coupling is disengaged and the wagons run forward.

The Swannington engine is a long-stroke, single expansion engine with a cylinder 18$\frac{1}{4}$ in. in diameter and of 3 ft. 6 in. stroke, and a piston valve; it drives through a single reversing gear a square shaft to which is fixed the winding drum and the brake for lowering.

At one period it was advocated that the Liverpool & Manchester Railway, opened on 15 September 1830, should be worked throughout its length by fixed engines and rope haulage, but a pamphlet by Robert Stephenson and Joseph Locke and the success of the *Rocket* at the locomotive trials at Rainhill in October 1829, settled the matter in favour of locomotives. The only stationary engines, therefore, were at the Liverpool end. The first passenger station in Liverpool, at Crown Street, was approached by a rising incline from Edge Hill, worked by a rope and stationary engine. A more accessible terminus, in Lime Street, replaced it in 1836. The approach to it was also rope-worked from Edge Hill, but in the eastbound direction only, up a gradient of 1 in 93. Westbound trains ran down by gravity to the terminus. This form of working lasted until March 1870, when locomotive haulage was substituted.

The first goods station in Liverpool, at Wapping, was reached on a falling gradient from Edge Hill of 1 in 48. Stationary engines at Edge Hill, one on each side of the Moorish Arch originally built there, hauled trains up to Edge Hill by endless hempen rope. The man in charge rode on the front wagon holding the messenger rope. A steel rope was soon substituted and more powerful engines were installed. Rope haulage was used until 11 May 1896. A steel rope was used from August 1849 to 16 February 1895, on a section of the line from Edge Hill to the Waterloo goods station, Liverpool.

For the first few years trains were hauled by cable up the incline from Euston Station to Camden. This is $1\frac{1}{4}$ miles long and rises at gradients of 1 in 70, 1 in 112 and 1 in 77, necessitated by the need to pass under the Hampstead Road almost at the start and over the Regent's Canal at Camden Town. George Stephenson advocated its operation by stationary engine and rope instead of by assisting engine. The first section of the London & Birmingham Railway, to Boxmoor, was opened on 20 July 1837 but as the two 60 h.p. winding engines on order from Maudslay, Sons & Field were not ready, trains were locomotive-hauled up the incline until 14 October 1837. Locomotives were detached at Chalk Farm from up trains, which were lowered thence into Euston; their speed was controlled by brakesmen called "bank-riders". Trains were pulled from Euston up the incline at 20 m.p.h., a whistle communicated by pneumatic tube signifying to the man in charge of the winding engine that they were ready to start. The rope was 4,080 yd. long and 3 in. thick.

The winding engines were housed in a large engine house just north of the Regent's Canal Bridge and the line was flanked there by two very tall chimney stacks to carry away the smoke of the steam-raising furnaces. It is said that the proprietor of a new tavern in the neighbourhood advertised proudly that his windows commanded a view of these chimneys.

Rope haulage was given up on 14 July 1844. The rope was sold back to the makers and the winding engines eventually found a new home in a Russian mine.

The opposition of the Forth & Clyde Canal Company forced the Edinburgh & Glasgow Railway to abandon its original proposal for a high-level terminus in Glasgow in favour of a low-level station in Queen Street, approached by a down gradient of 1 in 41–43 for 1¼ miles, mostly in tunnels, from Cowlairs.

The locomotives of ascending trains were assisted by rope, which imparted extra haulage power. At the top the rope was detached by a messenger rope without stopping the train. The winding mechanism at Cowlairs was controlled by signals given by the locomotive whistle. Special brake vans were attached on the journey down the incline.

At the opening of the line on 21 February 1842 a hempen rope was used, but this was subsequently replaced by an endless steel cable. Despite this and the cost of the frequent renewals involved, cable working was not abandoned until 1 April 1909, when banking engines at the rear of ascending trains were substituted. Even in the 1840s some heavy banking locomotives had been built to replace the cable but had damaged the road.

The Düsseldorf–Elberfeld line was opened to Erkrath, five miles, at the end of 1838 and throughout in 1841. Robert Stephenson advised on the route taken, 16¾ miles long, with a total rise of 392 ft. A continuous incline of 1 in 30 was made between Erkrath and Hochdahl, 1¾ miles, and stationary engines used. The line was single at first, but Wiebe, the engineer, soon doubled it and used a locomotive descending the gradient to haul on the cable and assist the ascending train. There were then three tracks on the incline. This system of working lasted until 1927. At first, pneumatic signalling between the two stations indicated when the cable was made fast and the train was to be set in motion.

A remarkable line, engineered by J. Jessop, was opened to link the Cromford Canal at Cromford with the Peak Forest Canal at Whaley Bridge. It was boldly laid through the heart of the Peak District, reaching a summit level of 1,264 ft. at Ladmanlow, near Buxton. Not all the line remains in use, and some other sections have been realigned.

Originally there were nine cable-worked inclines, of which the two steepest, at Bunsall, inclined at 1 in 7½ and 1 in 7, were abandoned in 1892. The only two still cable-operated are Sheep Pasture (near Cromford), ¾-mile long and 1 in 8–9, and Middleton (double track 800 yd. long and 1 in 8¼), where the winding house has the beam engine supplied by the Butterley Iron Works Company (now the Butterley Co. Ltd.) in 1825 and still largely in its original condition. It is a twin-cylinder condensing beam engine with a working pressure of 5 lb. p.s.i. The cylinders are 2 ft. 1 in. dia. × 5 ft. stroke. Although the two Lancashire boilers supplying steam are of later date, they are fed by the original feed pump. A pinion of 5 ft. pitch dia. in the crank shaft engages with a spur wheel 13 ft. 9½ in. in pitch diameter, giving a gear ratio of 2·75 to 1. The spur wheel is attached to a wire rope pulley with two grooves and 14 ft. 1 in. in diameter. Another similar pulley above guides the incoming rope, the arrangement ensuring that no reverse bend occurs in it.

The Hopton incline, with a gradient of 1 in 14, was operated by a beam engine until about 1880. It is now worked by adhesion. It is said to have been the scene of the first trials of the Fell centre-rail system in 1863–65 (see Chapter Two), and it was certainly that of another interesting experiment a few years later, when an ingenious rope system devised by Handysides of Derby was temporarily substituted for the existing stationary engine haulage. In this a locomotive itself became the winder. It was fitted with a long wire rope wound on a drum hung beneath the footplate; the drum was worked through gears by separate cylinders. To the loose end of wire rope was attached a special vehicle fitted with clips, which gripped the rails. The engine ascended the incline alone, paying out rope, the 200 yd. length of which allowed it to go halfway up. It was then clipped to the rails and hauled up the rope with the special vehicle to which two loaded vehicles were attached. When these were brought up to the engine, the clips on the special vehicle were fastened to the rails. The locomotive then climbed to the top, again paying out the rope, and the operation was repeated. The method was slow, and it was found that by taking a run an ordinary locomotive could haul up two or three wagons. This practice has been continued ever since.

The Brussels–Liège main line of the Belgian National Railways, now electrified, descends from Ans to Liège-Guillemins at 1 in 32. This section was opened on 1 May 1842, with cable operation. It was divided halfway, at Haut-Pré, where there was an engine house with four 80 h.p. engines. Both sets of engines could drive either cable at will. Sixty-ton trains could be hauled at $12\frac{1}{2}$ m.p.h. The cables, supported by pulleys between the rails, were formed of eight threads of iron wire and were more than 1 in. thick. In October 1843 the Ans–Liège line became part of an international route between Brussels and Cologne. Cable traction continued until 1866 for all trains and until September 1871 for freight trains.

One of the earliest railways in London, the London & Blackwall, was originally cable-worked over its whole length of $3\frac{1}{2}$ miles. The choice was made because of the nearness of the stations and the danger to the roofs of the houses along the route from burning locomotive coke.

As the Commercial Railway, it was authorised on 28 July 1836. Robert Stephenson and George Bidder were the engineers. The original London terminus was in the

Minories, and the railway extended eastward to Blackwall, 3¼ miles. Almost as soon as the Act was obtained
it was recognised that the terminus in the Minories was
not sufficiently near to the heart of the City, and it was
proposed, unsuccessfully, to extend to Lime Street. In
1837 a ¼-mile extension was sanctioned to a terminus
off Fenchurch Street and the title of the railway was
changed to the London & Blackwall.

The extension to Fenchurch Street was built on a
rising gradient of 1 in 150, so that departing trains
could travel by gravity to the Minories, where they
were attached to the rope. In the up direction the
gradient was considered sufficient to dissipate the momentum attained by the trains before reaching the
Minories. At Blackwall also the ropes were detached
and attached outside the terminus, and the final section was also on a rising gradient of 1 in 150 for the
same purpose as at Fenchurch Street. The line, laid to
the 5 ft. 1 in. gauge, was built on a brick viaduct to the
West India Dock Road, thence on an embankment, and
finally in a shallow cutting.

The stationary engines for working the line were in
duplicate, used in turn. As the line rose 68 ft. between
Blackwall and the Minories, the engines at the Minories, having to haul the trains up the gradient, were each
of 224 h.p.: those at Blackwall were only 140 h.p. each.
Each line had its own rope, the length of which was
more than twice the distance between engine houses.
The ropes were wound over a drum at one end and
under one at the other. The drums were 23 ft. in diameter and 3 ft. 8 in. wide. The engines were of the condensing (vacuum) type. Five boilers were provided for
each set of engines, two Cornish and three marine, also
used in turn. The motion was conveyed from the engine to the drums by spur wheels. The drums from each
line were on the same shaft; when one was being

wound, the other was being unwound, by the engine at the other end, and was disconnected from the shaft, as it was necessarily revolved in the contrary direction.

The ropes were supported by cast-iron sheaves 3 in. in diameter, placed between each pair of rails, and about 33 ft. apart; there were 493 of them for each pair of metals, as well as three wooden rollers at the Minories and two at Blackwall. The ropes were at first of hemp, 5¾ in. in circumference, and weighed about 40 tons each. The Cooke & Wheatstone electric telegraph was installed for signalling between the engine houses and the stations, the first time that it had formed part of the equipment of a railway from the outset.

There were first class, first/third composite, and third class coaches, all six wheelers. Two guards rode on a platform at one end of each carriage. They disconnected the carriages from the train at different stations and threw off the rope by means of an apparatus on the platform of each carriage. There were seven carriages in a train. On leaving Fenchurch Street the train travelled by gravity to the Minories where it was attached to the rope. The first two carriages, a third and a first class, went through to Blackwall. The remainder were composites; the rear one in turn was detached at each station without the train stopping by the guard withdrawing the pin from the coupling. Each coach was stopped by handbrake. Thus the seventh carriage came off at Shadwell, the sixth at Stepney, fifth at Limehouse, fourth at East India Docks, and third at Poplar, and all stations had a non-stop service from the City.

A mixed carriage had also left Stepney and a similar one left Shadwell for Blackwall. These coaches started as soon as the rope began to move and were non-stop to the terminus, where they arrived one in advance of the other, the interval being the time the second coach took to travel between Shadwell and Stepney; the Shadwell coach preceded the train by the amount of time which that train took to travel between the Minories and Shadwell. The minimum number of coaches on the rope was therefore nine. The whole journey took 13 minutes compared with 16 minutes later by steam with seven intermediate stops.

In the reverse direction, carriages started from each station for Fenchurch Street simultaneously, arriving at intervals. Four coaches left Blackwall, two running through and one being dropped at Stepney and one at Shadwell. The trains left each terminus at the same time at intervals of 15 minutes. Each line was used alternately for up and down trains. In summer the service was from 8 a.m. to 10 p.m. amd in winter from 8.30 a.m. to 9 p.m.

As the hemp ropes broke frequently, wire ropes, weighing about 100 tons each and used with swivels about every 800 yd. to avoid twisting, superseded them. The line was converted to steam traction and 4 ft. $8\frac{1}{2}$ in. gauge when a connection with the Eastern Counties Railway was planned. Rope haulage had ceased by 31 March 1849.

The first tube railway in London was cable-worked, and ran under the Thames from Great Tower Hill to Vine Street, Southwark, a distance of 1,340 ft. It originated with Peter William Barlow, who thought that cast-iron cylinders might be driven horizontally under rivers as successfully as they were used vertically for bridge piers. The Tower Subway Company was incorporated in 1868 and began work early in 1869. Barlow was the designer, and his assistant, James Henry Greathead, the contractor.

A shield of wrought and cast iron was designed by Barlow. The single tunnel was lined with cast-iron rings formed from segments and giving an internal diameter of 7 ft. A flat-bottom track of 2 ft. 6 in. gauge was laid. There were level sections at the termini and under the centre of the river, connected by 1 in 29 inclines. The rails were 66 ft. below high water level at the deepest part.

The formal opening was on 2 August 1870, although the line had then been working experimentally for several months. A single four-wheel car, 10 ft. long and seating 14 passengers, was attached by a gripper to a steel cable which ran over a drum worked by a stationary engine at each end of the line. Separate engines worked the cage-type lifts, worked on the counterbalance principle, at the termini. The line was shortlived because of mechanical troubles, and the tunnel was adapted to serve as a pedestrian subway, being opened as such on 24 December 1870. In this form it gave useful service until made redundant by the opening of the Tower Bridge in 1894. It now carries hydraulic power cables and water mains.

Barlow's idea of tube construction, as realised by Greathead, was proved feasible and appeared to offer a more economical means of constructing underground railways than the sub-surface, cut-and-cover method used in building the Metropolitan and Metropolitan District lines. The first tube railway proper was the City & Southwark Subway, authorised in 1884, and opened in 1890 as the City & South London Railway. It was originally to be operated by two ropes. One was to run from the engine house near the Elephant & Castle along the up line to the City (King William Street), returning along the down line; the other was to run from the engine house to Stockwell, the southern terminus, and back. The leading car of each train was to carry a cable gripper. Before the line was opened, however, it was decided to adopt electric traction instead.

The next cable line for passengers in Britain was the tramway up Highgate Hill, London, opened in 1884, and the first cable tramway in Europe. San Francisco pioneered the cable tram in 1873 and this system of transport enjoyed a considerable vogue, particularly where topography made horse or steam traction on tramways difficult if not impossible. Despite the subsequent widespread electrification of tramways some systems, Edinburgh and Melbourne, for example, remained cable-worked for many years.

Apart from the short-lived Tower Subway, the only cable-worked underground railway in this country was that opened at Glasgow by the Glasgow District Subway Company on 14 December 1896, more than six years after it had been authorised. Although, as stated, the City & South London was electrically worked, opinions by no means unanimously favoured the newer form of traction, and the merits and demerits of both continued to be argued for some years. Native caution prevailed at all events in Scotland.

The Glasgow Subway, as it was long known, is circular, 6 miles 44 chains long, from St. Enoch *via* Bridge Street, Cessnock, Govan, Partick, Kelvin Bridge, Cowcaddens, and Buchanan Street, back to St. Enoch. The inner and outer lines are not connected, and run in separate 11-ft. dia. tunnels which merge into one large tunnel at stations, all of which have island platforms. Cut-and-cover construction, shield working under compressed air, and boring under air pressure without a shield were all used. The line passes under the River Clyde twice.

Two Corliss horizontal non-condensing engines, with single cylinders of 42-in. dia. and 6-ft. stroke, developed 1,500 h.p. Their 25-ft. flywheels weighed 50 tons each. The engines could be used singly or coupled. Drums 13 ft. 9 in. in diameter drove four 25-ft. dia. drums mounted on the cable drum shaft. From the shaft, four Walker's differential drums drove the 2-in. cables. Winches maintained the tension.

The railway was bought by Glasgow Corporation on 1 August 1923. Electrification was discussed in 1925 and again in 1932, and finally carried out in 1935, on the Inner Circle on 31 March and the Outer on 5 December. The narrowness of the tunnels and of the gauge, which is the unusual one of 4 ft., made the conversion difficult, but the service was maintained throughout. The existing rolling stock was modified for electric working.

It can hardly be contested that the most spectacular example of cable working remaining is to be found on the Santos–Jundiai Railway in Brazil, formerly, under British ownership, the San Paulo Railway. The city of São Paulo lies not far inland from the Atlantic seaport of Santos, but between the two rises the great rampart of the Serra do Mar, broken by no pass.

In 1856, the Baron de Maua obtained from Dom Pedro II, the Emperor of Brazil, a concession to build a railway from Santos to São Paulo and Jundiai, in the rich State of São Paulo. Far and away the most difficult task confronting the projectors was the scaling of the precipitous Serra. The whole line, 83½ miles long, was to be built to the 5 ft. 3 in. gauge, and to main line standards, at a total cost of not more than £2,000,000. The British railway engineer Brunlees accepted the challenge and deputed one of his former pupils, Daniel Makinson Fox, an engineer of only 26, who had already built mountain railways in the Pyrenees and North Wales, to carry out the work.

No more thankless task can have awaited an engineer. Not only is the Serra composed of granite and rubble, but it is also thickly forested and subject to torrential rain. It cost Fox many months of heart-

(*Photo: J. R. Day*)

View from cab of descending car,
Pilatus Railway; ascending car about
to pass over traversing points.

(*Photo: Swiss National Tourist Office*)

Jungfrau Railway train descending
from Jungfraujoch.

(*Below*)   Handyside locomotive tried on the Hopton incline of the Cromford
and High Peak Railway, Derbyshire.

(*Above*)   Crossing place on cable-worked inclines up the Serra do Mar, Santos-Jundiai (former San Paulo) Railway.

(*Below*)   Two parallel cable-worked inclines on the Serra do Mar section of the Santos-Jundiai Railway. Note the series of tunnels and elaborate defences against washouts.

breaking toil before he discovered a route which was remotely practicable, and even this entailed climbing more than 2,500 ft. in five miles. The rack system had not then been developed, and zigzags were out of the question because of the cost. Fox thereupon proposed to Brunlees to divide the slope into four inclines, 5,842, 6,388, 6,876 and 7,017 ft. long, each with a gradient of 1 in 9·75, and to be worked by cables. Between each incline there was to be a 250 ft. section of 1 in 75, the bankhead, where a cable power house was to be built. Brunlees approved, and the San Paulo (Brazilian) Railway Co. Ltd., formed in London, began construction.

The building of the inclines was hampered by torrential rains, landslides and the crumbling nature of the rock. Massive masonry works had to be erected and deep gulleys dug. No tunnels but many bridges were required.

The need to keep down costs dictated the choice of the tail-end system of rope haulage, subsequently used on funicular railways, in which one end of the rope is attached to the ascending and the other to the descending train, thereby reducing the amount of stationary engine power needed. It also caused Fox to adopt a three-rail layout, with the centre rail used by both up and down trains, opening out to four only at passing loops. At the bankheads were erected engine houses to accommodate two 150-h.p. steam engines, with 10-ft. dia. wheels to take the cables.

The railway was opened throughout in 1867. In 1895, so greatly had traffic increased, it was decided to double the line between Jundiai and the summit of the Serra and duplicate the Serra section. The cable system worked so well that it was used also on the five new inclines, each 1·34 miles long. To reduce the gradient to 1 in 12½, 16 viaducts and 13 tunnels were built. On the new inclines also the three-rail arrangement with passing loops was adopted, but the continuous rope system was chosen. The original inclines are still used by goods trains when necessary.

When a train from Santos reaches Piassaguera at the foot of the range, or one from São Paulo reaches Alto da Serra at the top, the locomotive is detached, and the train divided into sections, each weighing not more than 89 tons. Each section is then propelled to the end of the initial stage by an 0–4–0 locomotive called a locomotive-brake which grips the rope and transmits its pull to the train. This locomotive has both the automatic vacuum brake, and rail-grip brakes for descent. It has also enough tractive power to shunt the 89-ton train sections along the level tracks between inclines. When each locomotive-brake has lifted the rope and gripped it, the drivers touch a wire beside the track to advise the winding house that their train is ready. Trains on all five stages start simultaneously, so that there are five ascending and five descending when the incline works normally.

Five hauling engines are situated under the track at the bankheads, and the wire rope for hauling the sections or trains up and letting them down the incline enters each engine house from the up line and makes four turns round the rope wheels, passing to a 14-ft. dia. return wheel at the back of the power house and passing out thence to down line. Each rope, of $5\frac{1}{4}$ in. circumference, has a resistance to breaking of 104 tons when new; it is renewed by the time wear has reduced it to 84 tons. It passes underground at the foot of each stage, where a tension slide and tension weight of 6 tons return it from one line to another and keep it taut over the pulleys. It is claimed that the rope splicers employed are the most expert in the world.

On the old incline loads of 2,400 tons were taken up

daily and 1,800 tons brought down. The new inclines, with their 1,000-h.p. Corliss engines, handled average daily loads of 11,700 tons up and 9,500 down. Since the railway was taken over by Brazil in 1946, the cables on the new line have been electrically worked. After the first world war it was proposed to supersede the inclines by a new electric line following a longer but flatter route, and but for a change of Government in the 1930s the plan might have been carried out. The project has been revived in the last few years, but the cost rules it out at present. Meanwhile the cable inclines continue to give wonderful service, a monument to one of the most successful Anglo-Brazilian technical ventures.

Until it fell victim to the depression of the early 1930s an unusual inclined plane railway operated at Mauch Chunk (now Jim Thorpe), Pennsylvania, a town on the Lehigh River, encircled by the Blue Ridge Mountains.

In 1818 a road was made to bring coal from Summit Hill to the Lehigh River at Mauch Chunk and rails were laid on it in 1827. The wagons ran down by gravity; the empty wagons were returned to the mines by mules which rode down with the coal but in their own wagon. In 1844, to obviate the use of mules, a second route was laid out from Mauch Chunk over Mount Pisgah and Mount Jefferson, with cable-worked inclined planes up each, to Summit Hill, where the original route was rejoined.

The line was abandoned as a means of coal transport in 1870 and converted by the town into a pleasure railway, the Mauch Chunk Switch-Back. Except for the two inclined planes (Mount Pisgah 2,322 ft. long and Mount Jefferson 2,070 ft.) the 18-mile round trip through rugged picturesque country was performed by gravity. On the final section of the gravity descent, averaging 96 ft. to the mile, from Summit Hill to Mauch

Chunk, a speed of 50-60 m.p.h. was reached. The cables of the inclines were wound on 28 ft. dia. drums and connected to small tractors to which the open-sided cars were coupled for the ascent.

CHAPTER FOUR

FUNICULARS

AS its name implies, the funicular is merely a special type of rope railway and has been applied to short independent lines on which the gradient is considered too steep for a rack. Two cars are linked by a steel cable which runs round a winding wheel at the upper terminus. When the weights of the cars are adjusted that of the descending car lifts the other car. The line may be double all the way, or single or "gauntletted" with a crossing place at the halfway point.

There are many examples in the world, from the line which rises behind Bergen, in Norway, to those up the Peak on Penang Island and to the summit of Mount Rokko San, in Japan. Nowhere have they been developed more than in Switzerland, the country *par excellence* of diversity in transport. It can claim more than 50 funicular railways, of great variety. The steepest, and probably the steepest railways of any type in the world, are the Piotta-Piora, or Ritom, in Canton Ticino, and the Châtelard-Barberine. Both were built to convey materials for the building of hydro-electric power-stations of the Swiss Federal Railways. The Ritom line rises 1,487 yd. with a maximum gradient of 88 per cent, and the Barberine line almost equals it with a length of 1,433 yd. and its steepest pitch at 87 per cent. They have been adapted for passenger transport. The longest Swiss funicular climbs from Sierre, in the Rhone Valley, up to Montana, 4,652 yd., and because of its length is divided, like some others, into two separate sections; the Stanserhorn funicular, in Central

Switzerland, has three sections, totalling 4,310 yd. The
Davos-Parsenn line, in the Grisons, well-known in
particular to devotees of winter sports, is not only the
highest Swiss funicular, with a summit level of 8,737 ft.,
but it also operates two-car trains, seating 140.

Lightweight construction has enabled not only more
capacious cars to be provided on some of these cable
lines but also the speed to be raised to as much as 11
m.p.h. As on rack railways, the safety precautions
are elaborate. Most Swiss funiculars are electrically
worked, but some are worked on the water-balance
principle. The most easily-graded is operated by water
turbines, the urban line from Ouchy, on the Lake of
Geneva, to Lausanne above; the steepest section is 1 in
13, so that three- and sometimes four-car trains may be
run. This railway, one of the busiest urban funiculars
anywhere, was opened in 1877, and has contributed
greatly to the growth of Lausanne. It is 1½ km. long,
about one-third in tunnel. Normally, a water turbine is
used but when water is short a standby steam engine is
called on. The upper terminus is at Flon, a commercial
quarter of Lausanne, where the railway has a depot.
Lower down, the line passes under the Swiss Federal
Railways main station (Gare CFF). Formerly the
"main" line of the funicular was paralleled by a second
line, using the same tunnel, but conveying wagons only,
from Flon to the goods station of the Swiss Federal
Railways. In 1953 this goods station was removed to
the western suburb of Sébeillon, which was linked to
Flon by a new Federal Railways spur. The Flon–Gare
CFF parallel line, which like the Ouchy line is cable-
worked but also has the Riggenbach rack for braking,
now operates a useful shuttle for passengers, carrying
some 650,000 a year compared with 3,000,000 for the
Flon–Ouchy line.

The Ouchy line normally operates two three-car

trains, with a spare car for peak periods, and owns 30 wagons, mainly to handle the considerable traffic in coal to the lake steamers at Ouchy. Because of this need for through working of wagons the normal funicular practice of double-flanged outside wheels and flangeless inner wheels could not be followed.

In recent years suspension lines (*téléphériques*) and chair lifts have come increasingly into favour in Switzerland and other mountainous countries, but although they work on the same principle as funiculars they differ in that the cars are suspended from a cable instead of being hauled on rails by it. They therefore fall outside the scope of this book

One of the familiar features of Paris is the funicular railway which has climbed the slopes of Montmartre from the Square Saint-Pierre to Basilique since 13 July 1900. This line is now owned by the Paris transport authority (*Régie Autonome des Transports Parisiens*). It was rebuilt in 1934–35, when water–ballast working was replaced by electric. Other well-known funiculars in France include those at Marseilles, Lyons, Cannes, and Lourdes. The inclined lifts which rise to stages 1 and 2 of the Eiffel Tower, Paris, almost merit inclusion in this category also.

A veteran urban funicular exists at Istanbul. A concession was granted by the Imperial Ottoman Government to a Monsieur Gavaud for 42 years, and the Metropolitan Railway of Constantinople, from Galata to Pera, Limited, formed in England on 22 June 1872. The line, opened with considerable ceremony on 17 January 1875, runs from the shipping and commercial quarter of Galata, the lower terminus, to the residential area of Pera. It is only 672 yd. long, of which 634 yd. are in tunnel. The rise is 200 ft. and the average gradient 1 in 10. The greatest depth is 80 ft. The line is double track with balancing cars.

Although Britain cannot match some of the funicular railways abroad, it has some inclined cliff railways of funicular type, less correctly called cliff lifts, which well deserve description. The first to be opened was the standard-gauge line up the South Cliff, Scarborough, from the foreshore to the Esplanade. It began working in 1874. The rise is 284 ft. and the gradient 1 in 1·75. Until converted to electric traction between 1933 and 1935, it was worked by filling a water-ballast tank under the car at the upper station so that the extra weight would enable it on descending to haul up the other car, by a cable passing round a headwheel at the top, a system which has continued in use on some lines.

The second such line was also at Scarborough, the Central Tramway, opened in 1880. It is 255 ft. long, from the Grand Hotel to the South Foreshore Road. Steam was used until the early 1900s, when a 500 V. d.c. motor was substituted. This and the control room are housed beneath the tracks, about halfway up the cliff, and the operator has to rely on a colliery-type indicator. On 2 June 1884, a 207-ft. cliff railway was opened at Saltburn, Yorkshire, to replace a vertical lift. The line is of 4 ft. 2½ in. gauge and is on a gradient of 1 in 1·85. The water-balance system is used.

The Folkestone Lift Company opened the first cliff railway in Southern England on 16 September 1885, from the front to the Leas at Folkestone. In 1890 this, a 5 ft. 10 in. gauge line, was duplicated by another double-track line with a gauge of 4 ft. 10 in., laid immediately to the west. Both are water-operated. The cars on the later line have stepped floors, but in those of the earlier line the floor is level and mounted on a triangular underframe, as is more usual. Another similar lift, further west along the Leas, owned by the Folkestone Metropole Lift Co. Ltd., was opened on 31

March 1904. Its use was discontinued during the second world war and it has been dismantled.

The longest and most interesting cliff railway in Britain links the North Devon resorts of Lynton and Lynmouth, and was opened on 1 April 1890. The line rises 901 ft., at 1 in 2, in a wooded cutting through the rock. The space between the two 3 ft. 6 in. gauge tracks is insufficient for the cars to pass except at the halfway point, originally an intermediate station, where it widens for a short distance. The cars are linked by cables passing over pulleys at both the top and bottom of the incline. Water is piped from the West Lyn River to storage tanks at the upper (Lynton) terminus. After use it is discharged into the sea at Lynmouth. To allow for easy inspection and painting, the car bodies, which seat 16, are detachable and may be run off the under-carriage on flanged wheels into a car shed. The railway is unusual in having driver-conductors.

The first of the two cliff railways at Hastings, the West Hill funicular, was opened in 1891 by the Hastings Passenger Lift Co. Ltd. It is 500 ft. long, from George Street to the top of the hill near the Castle ruins, rising at 1 in 3. The gauge is 5 ft. $8\frac{1}{2}$ in. The railway, which is municipally owned, runs mostly in a tunnel, 19 ft. wide by 18 ft. high, in part a natural tunnel enlarged. A Tangye 32-h.p. diesel engine has replaced the 40-h.p. Crossley gas engine which originally supplied power. A funicular up the East Cliff, Hastings, dates from 9 April 1903, and is owned by the Corporation. It is 192 ft. long, and has a gradient of 1 in $1\frac{1}{2}$. The gauge is 5 ft. between rail centres.

There is only one remaining British funicular railway inland, the Castle Hill Railway at Bridgnorth, Shropshire. It is 201 ft. long, inclined at 1 in $1\frac{3}{4}$, and links the Old Town with the lower New Town. To avoid spoiling the scenery, the line was made in a cutting 50 ft. into the sandstone and special care was taken in the excavation to avoid damage to houses below. From its opening on 7 July 1892, to December 1944, it was worked by water-balance, but is now electric. The rails are flat-bottom, laid to the 3 ft. 8½ in. gauge. In June 1955, the 1892 cars were replaced by new vehicles of pleasing design.

A line, now owned by the proprietors of the Pier Pavilion, was opened on 1 August 1896 from the promenade at Aberystwyth to the top of Constitution Hill. The incline is 1 in 2 at its steepest part. Toast-rack cars with stepped floor are used. This line also was converted from water-balance to electric operation. The Isle of Man has three incline railways—at Douglas Head, Port Soderick (now derelict), and Falcon Cliff Hotel, Douglas. The first and second are worked by oil engine, but the third is electric, with overhead current collection.

Sir George Newnes, who promoted the Lynton-Lynmouth cliff railway and was the first chairman of the Bridgnorth Castle Hill Railway Co. Ltd., unsuccessfully projected a funicular at Babbacombe, Torquay, where one was eventually built by the National Electric Construction Co. Ltd. for the Torquay Tramways Co. Ltd. It was opened on 1 April 1926 and was acquired by Torquay Corporation in April 1935. The line, which connects Babbacombe with Oddicombe Beach, was closed on 16 October 1941 and reopened on 29 June 1951, after reconstruction. It is 718 ft. long and inclined at 1 in 2·84; 35-lb. flat-bottom rails are used, spiked to transverse sleepers, which rest on longitudinal reinforced-concrete beams.

Another venture of Sir George Newnes was the Clifton Rocks Railway at Bristol, from Hotwells on the Avon to the eastern end of the Clifton Suspension Bridge. It was opened on 11 March 1893, and was well patronised for many years, until the bus services operated by the Bristol Tramways & Carriage Co. Ltd., which took over the line on 29 November 1912, caused the traffic to decline, and enforced its closure on 1 October 1934. Four tracks were laid, although except at busy periods only two cars were used. They rose 200 ft. at a gradient of 1 in 2½, through a 27-ft. by 18-ft. tunnel. Difficulties encountered in the rock strata increased the cost of construction from the £10,000 estimated to £40,000. In 1940 the tunnels were skilfully adapted to form an emergency headquarters for the British Broadcasting Corporation.

A much shorter-lived line, which opened in the same year, was the Sandgate Hill Railway, from the western end of Sandgate Hill up to the western end of the Leas, Folkestone, near the Martello Tower. It began running in February 1893, and closed in July 1918. The line, worked on the hydraulic counterbalance system, was of 5 ft. 6 in. gauge and rose 670½ ft. on gradients of 1 in 4·75, 1 in 7·04 and 1 in 4·75 again. The cars were individually controlled.

A still more brief existence was enjoyed by the 3 ft. 6 in. gauge Brighton Dyke Steep Grade Railway, opened on 24 July 1897, and closed about 1908. The line climbed from Poynings to the top of the Devils Dyke, a distance of 840 ft., on varying gradients, of which the steepest was 1 in 1·5. It consisted of flat-bottom 35 lb. rails laid on longitudinal timbers. There were two 14-seat cars with open sides and power was provided by a 25 h.p. Hornsby-Ackroyd oil engine.

Although other funiculars have been proposed in Britain, as at Malvern and Ventnor, the only others built and in use are the short cliff railways at Bournemouth and Southend.

CHAPTER FIVE

ATMOSPHERIC RAILWAYS

IN 1810–12 George Medhurst published a plan for "conveying letters and goods by air". His proposal, expounded in detail in a pamphlet published in 1827, was for an airtight tunnel with carriages, running on iron rails, almost fitting it and moved piston-wise by air forced in from behind. Exhaustion of the air in front of the carriage would enable it to travel in the opposite direction. Alternatively he suggested a pipe carrying a piston carriage, which could convey goods, with a rod leading out of it through a valve to a passenger car. This method could be applied to a road vehicle except that the pipe would be smaller and the piston merely a propelling agent. The valve might be of thin sheets of iron or copper shutting on to a soft substance to form an airtight joint.

Medhurst is said in some accounts to have been a Dane, a mistake arising from the fact that he once lived in Denmark Street, London. An earlier idea of his, also far in advance of his day, was to propel road coaches by compressed air stored in cylinders beneath them. The cylinders would have been re-charged or changed at "filling stations" along the highways.

A Mr. Vallance proposed to carry passengers along a line laid wholly within an airtight tunnel built of cast-iron or vitrified clay. As in Medhurst's system, the creation of a vacuum in front of the carriage would "suck" it along. A demonstration at Brighton proved the idea practicable, but the notion of being sucked through a dark, close tunnel made no popular appeal, particularly as Vallance considered it applicable to a railway between London and Brighton.

In 1835 Henry Pinkus, an American living in London, was granted a patent for an invention " by means whereof Carriages or Cars may be Propelled on Railways, and Vessels may be Propelled on Canals". He proposed a cast-iron tube 3–4 ft. in diameter, with a 1–2 in. wide slit along the top. Two cheeks, cast with the tube, lay along the sides of the opening, forming a channel 4–5 in. deep. The tube was made airtight by a "valvular cord of yielding substance". Inside the tube ran a piston car, or "dynamic traveller", pushed forward by air pressure behind it whenever the action of pumps created a partial vacuum in front. This piston was connected by a bar passing through the slit to the haulage vehicle, or "governor" running on rails. A device lifted the valve to allow the bar to travel along and when the bar had passed returned the valve to its seat and lubricated its sides.

At first Pinkus intended to make the tube large enough for the wheels of trains to run on rails or ledges cast outside it, but a rise in the price of cast-iron caused him to reduce it to a diameter of about 10 in. and place it between stone blocks laid end to end. On these blocks rested iron bars instead of rails, their ends fitted into chairs supported on a pile interposed after every fourth block and linked by tiebars with the pipe.

Pinkus exhibited a working model in Cavendish Square and the National Pneumatic Railway Association was formed to exploit the system. In 1836 he obtained a second patent for improvements and laid down a full-size trial line near the Kensington Canal. He was at pains to show how the absence of locomotive shocks, which were said to have damaged the permanent way of the Liverpool & Manchester Railway, would enable vehicles to be lighter. Steeper gradients and greater speeds were possible, and the annual expenses of a pneumatic railway 30 miles long would be £47,782, or £33,770 less than those of an orthodox steam railway.

Pinkus's idea, although not directly successful, was taken up by others. In January 1839 Samuel Clegg and Jacob and Joseph Samuda patented a similar apparatus. The only difference from Pinkus's as far as *The Railway Magazine* (Herapath's) could see, was that one side of the valve was fastened down, a point on which, however, the inventors laid stress. Distinguished engineers like Cubitt and Vignoles, as well as the Council of the Institution of Civil Engineers, warmly approved. The trial apparatus was installed at Wormwood Scrubbs in 1840, and the French Academy of Sciences appointed a commission, including the politician-savant Arago, to examine the invention, but George Stephenson, after inspecting the scheme carefully, observed: "It won't do; it is only a modification of the fixed engine and ropes." The editor of *The Railway Magazine*, was who invited to a demonstration at Samuda's works at Southwark, foresaw some of the drawbacks of the system which later manifested themselves in practice—the difficulty of keeping the leather flap sound and free from undue wear caused by the motion of the arm, and the expense of laying the main tube and of erecting and maintaining the pumping stations.

The trial line at Wormwood Scrubbs comprised a 9-in. tube laid between contractor's rails which had been used on the Liverpool & Manchester Railway. Although the rails had been badly put down, a speed of 30 m.p.h. was obtained with more than five tons (a first class coach of the period weighed four tons) on a rising gradient of 1 in 120. This impressed the Dublin & Kingstown Railway directors sufficiently to induce them to adopt the system for their extension to Dalkey,

considered unsuitable for locomotives. The extension
had been built as a standard-gauge single line, 3,050 yd.
long, on the course of a stone quarry tramroad and included 365 yd. at 1 in 57 at the Dalkey end.

Vignoles was the engineer for the Dalkey atmospheric line, for which a 15-in. diameter pipe was
adopted. The slit ended 560 yd. from Dalkey, the pipe
continuing closed to the pumping station, and trains
took the steep section at a run, at least in theory! The
first trial took place on 19 August 1843 and at another,
in the presence of the Lord Lieutenant of Ireland,
three carriages are said to have ascended at the rate of
25 m.p.h. in 3 minutes, and returned by their own
momentum in 5 minutes. Public traffic began on 29
March 1844.

On the whole the system appears to have worked
fairly well on the Dalkey line, although it really applied
to one direction only, as trains coasted downhill. Locomotives were used from 23 December 1848 to 5 February 1849, while the air pump cylinder was repaired.
They were successful, but the company was content to
retain the atmospheric system until the line became
part of a through route. This it did in 1854 with the extension of the line to Bray, and on 12 April of that year
atmospheric working was abandoned and the equipment sold for scrap. The Kingstown–Dalkey line was
largely rebuilt, and the only reminder today of this
venture is the name of Atmospheric Road, Dalkey,
near the site of the original station.

Meanwhile the atmospheric principle gained many
notable adherents in England, and something like an
atmospheric mania set in. In March 1845 a Select
Committee was appointed to inquire into atmospheric
railways. Brunel and Vignoles, as well as Cubitt, the
engineer of the London & Croydon, which had decided
to try the system, gave evidence before it of their belief

that no difficulty would oppose its working whatever the length of line. Bidder, another railway engineer, and earlier famous as a "calculating boy", considered its mechanical problems solved and that the only question was its commercial application. Stephenson and Locke opposed it mainly because of the cost of keeping the apparatus efficient, though Stephenson had relented enough to admit that the longitudinal valve was "a complete triumph of mechanism". The Committee took a favourable view, considering that a single atmospheric line would be superior in regularity and safety to a double locomotive-worked line.

The London & Croydon Railway was opened on 1 June 1839, from a junction with the London & Greenwich at Corbets Lane, near New Cross, to what is now West Croydon, and was laid largely in the bed of the Croydon Canal. On Cubitt's advice it was decided to lay down a third pair of metals solely for atmospheric traction, in the first instance between Forest Hill and Croydon. The atmospheric line crossed over from the east to the west side of the steam lines at Norwood on a long flyover with inclines of 1 in 50, almost certainly the first flyover of any kind to be built.

Atmospheric traction was due to begin in June 1845 but trials did not begin until about two months later. A speed of 70 m.p.h. was reached with six coaches and 30 m.p.h. with 16 coaches. A tentative public service began on 27 October, with passengers carried free. From 19 January 1846 the Forest Hill–Croydon service was run entirely by atmospheric trains, and from 1 May both this service and that of the London Bridge–Forest Hill connecting steam trains were increased. The company's stock was then eight steam locomotives, 56 coaches, 89 wagons, six piston cars, and five heater cars (for use with atmospheric trains).

The atmospheric line was extended from Forest

(*Left*)
Mount Pisgah Plane on the former Mauch Chunk Switchback Railroad, Pennsylvania.

(*Below*)
Stationary engine house and ornamental chimneys at Camden Town, the top of the rope-worked incline from Euston, London & Birmingham Railway.

(*Photo: courtesy of British Transport Commission*)

(*Above*)   Cable mechanism of the Glasgow Subway (now electrified).

(*Below*)   Cable gripper of Glasgow Subway car.

(*Photos: courtesy of Glasgow Corporation*)

Hill to New Cross in time for experimental running early in 1846, and a third line was laid right up to Corbets Lane in expectation of the extension of atmospheric traction to London Bridge by widening the Greenwich Railway. Formal trips were run between Forest Hill and New Cross on 14 January 1847. The atmospheric line on this section was laid on the west side, with the result that trains had to cross the main lines again. The crossing was on the level, with a break in the pipes, over which atmospheric trains coasted. The Inspecting Officer of Railways refused to allow public traffic until a flyover was substituted.

Engine houses in a Gothic style were erected at Forest Hill and Norwood, and later also at New Cross and Croydon; the chimney of the Forest Hill house was 120 ft. high. Six boilers, each weighing about 14 tons, were installed in the first two houses.

Each of the four pumping engines on the line developed 50 h.p. Each tube section was distinct, with a self-acting valve opening in front of the piston and closing after it.

The Croydon Railway had gained authority to extend to Sutton and Epsom, and Cubitt decided to adopt atmospheric traction on this at an estimated cost of £200,000. He also advocated it for a London–Portsmouth line and one from Croydon to Maidstone, Tonbridge and Ashford. In 1845 the London & Croydon Railway promoted a Sydenham–Chatham atmospheric line, part of a Brunel scheme for a London, Chatham & Portsmouth Railway, of which the western part became the Portsmouth Atmospheric, from the Croydon–Epsom extension of the London & Croydon to Portsmouth *via* Dorking and Godalming. Where roads crossed the line on the level, it was proposed to have lifting bridges to be lowered across the line, clear of the tube, for road traffic to pass. Samuda's

6

royalty was to be £500 a mile. The Portsmouth Atmospheric was authorised, but the project lapsed.

Another atmospheric scheme of 1845 was the Windsor, Staines, Brentford & London Atmospheric Railway, which proposed a London terminus at Knightsbridge. The promoters, evidently hoping for royal patronage, stressed the "ample accommodation for transit" which would be afforded between Buckingham Palace and Windsor Castle.

At first, the atmospheric system on the London & Croydon worked well. In one test, two contiguous sections of tube, five miles long in all, were exhausted by a single engine, and trains were run at more than 60 m.p.h. over the double length. Trains were successfully started from rest at the foot of the Norwood flyover.

In the great heat of the summer of 1846, however, the valve sealing compound became too soft to retain the necessary solidity, and although this was remedied by the substitution of a harder composition, other defects showed themselves. On 27 July 1846 the London & Croydon and London & Brighton Railways amalgamated to form the London Brighton & South Coast Railway. The new company did not look with such favour on the atmospheric system and sought to abandon it because of expense. Samuda contended that the London Bridge–Epsom line could be operated atmospherically for 1s. 3d. a train mile compared with 1s. 11½d. with steam and contracted to work it for a fixed sum for a period. This offer was not taken up and on 4 May 1847 the L.B.S.C.R. dispensed with atmospheric working, which had never extended beyond Croydon, and sold much of the apparatus by auction. A total of £495,573 had been spent on the enterprise, including £2,500 for the patent, £4,309 for the Norwood flyover, £80,345 for permanent way, £42,778 for tubes

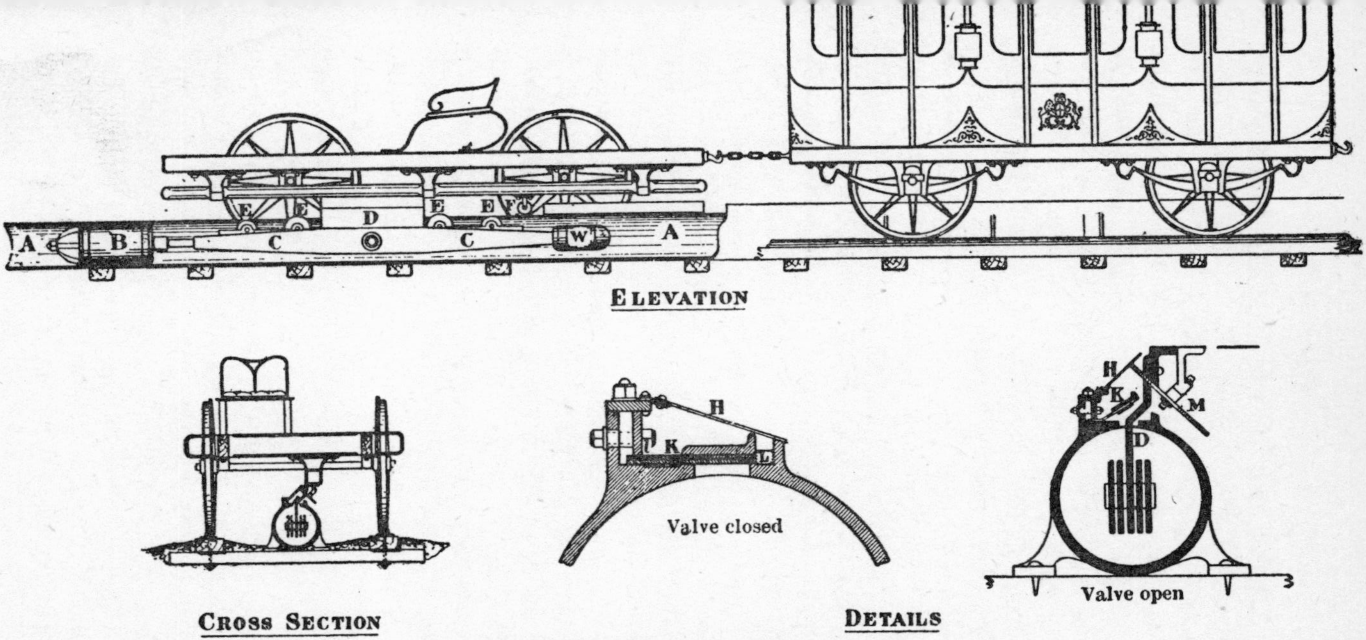
A
B
C
D
C
W
A
E
E
E
E
F
ELEVATION
CROSS SECTION
H
K
L
Valve closed
H
K
M
D
Valve open
DETAILS

THE ATMOSPHERIC SYSTEM

A.A. Continuous Pipe fixed between the rails.
B. Piston.
C.C. Iron Plates connected to the piston.
D. Plate connecting Apparatus to Carriage.
E. Metal Rollers to open the Continuous Valve.
F. Roller attached to Carriage for closing the Valve.
H. Weather Valve.[1]
K. Continuous Airtight Valve hinged at l.
L. Composition for sealing Valve.
M. Roller attached to Carriage for opening Weather Valve.[1]
W. Counterweight to Piston.

[1] These complications do not appear to have been in use on the South Devon Railway.

FIG. 2. The Clegg–Samuda atmospheric system

produced by permission of British Railways, Western Region, from History of the Great Western Railway *by E. T. MacDermot* and valves, £26,666 for pumping houses and engines, £966 for the electric telegraph, and £5,822 for "carriages" (presumably piston vehicles).

Before a description is given of the most spectacular application of the Clegg-Samuda system, that on the South Devon Railway, the following account of the principle may be helpful.

A 15-in. diameter cast-iron tube was laid between the running rails (22 in. was proposed for the steep inclines on the South Devon, to which the system was never extended). At intervals of about three miles were erected stationary engines, working large air pumps, by which air could be exhausted from the tube, and a partial vacuum created within it. When a close-fitting piston was placed in one end of the tube and the air was exhausted from the tube, the pressure of the external air on the surface of the piston which was towards the open end of the tube forced the piston through the tube towards the end where the air pumps were working. If therefore the piston were connected with a carriage running on the rails, it would draw the carriage with it.

Along the top of the tube was a slit, about $2\frac{1}{2}$ in. wide, closed by a long flap of leather—the longitudinal valve—which was strengthened with iron plates and secured to the tube at one side of the slit. On one side the leather thus formed a continuous hinge. The other edge, where it closed on the tube, was sealed with a composition of grease to make it airtight. When the valve was closed, air could be exhausted from the tube in the front of the piston and a partial vacuum formed. Behind the piston, the air being at atmospheric pressure within and outside the tube, there was no objection to opening the longitudinal valve. A bar or plate, extending downwards from the under side of the carriage, entered the slit obliquely under the opened valve and was connected to the rear end of a frame about 10 ft. long, the front end of which carried the piston. To allow the bar to pass along the slit, the valve was opened on its hinge, being pressed upwards by a series of wheels carried by the moving piston-frame inside the tube. The valve closed again after the train passed, being helped in this by a small roller on the carriage behind the plate. The tube was then ready to be exhausted in preparation for the passage of the next train. Another complication, a "weather valve", with a roller on the carriage to open it, does not seem to have been used on the South Devon. The waste of power caused by the heat of the air engendered and by the friction caused by its passage along the tube may have averaged something over 20 per cent of the work done.

Brunel, always eager to try out new devices, had been attracted to the atmospheric system from the start. As early as July 1840 he considered it for Box Tunnel, and subsequently conducted experiments himself at Wormwood Scrubbs and Dalkey. In 1843 he recommended it for part of the Genoa–Turin line, and in this instance Robert Stephenson, who thought the system mechanically sound but uneconomical, supported him. On 19 August 1844, as engineer of the South Devon Railway, which continued the 7-ft. gauge of the Great Western and Bristol & Exeter Railways from Exeter to Plymouth, Brunel recommended the directors to adopt it. At the first meeting of the company, on 28 August, it was announced that Samuda Brothers had proposed to apply their system, and that a deputation of directors had visited the Dalkey installation. These facts, and the "deliberate and very decided opinion" of Brunel had made the South Devon Board decide to adopt the system.

"I have no hesitation in taking upon myself the full and entire responsibility," said Brunel characteristically. The line was 52 miles long, but the cost of the atmospheric apparatus was taken on $41\frac{1}{2}$ only, as it was considered that auxiliary stationary power would be required in any case on the $10\frac{1}{2}$ miles of steep gradients. The earthworks were made sufficient for a single line only, except on two inclines.

In December 1844 Brunel prepared specifications and drawings of the steam engines and vacuum pumps. Tenders for six pairs of engines were accepted from Messrs. Boulton & Watt, Messrs. Rennie, and Messrs. Maudslay & Field. The engines, each of 12 h.p., were required to be high-pressure condensing, with double-seated expansion valves, and with boilers proved to 100 lb. p.s.i. and were guaranteed to work with safety valves loaded to 40 lb. p.s.i.

Cast-iron tubes were supplied by George Hennett at the rate of a mile a week. By mid-1846 almost the whole line was laid to Newton Abbot and the valve was ready to be fixed. Joseph Samuda and his assistants trained on the Croydon line went to Dawlish in the autumn. Because of delays in the erection of the engines and their houses it was not until February 1847 that a piston carriage was able to run the first six miles from Exeter. Brunel reported on 27 August 1847 that he regretted they had not yet been able to open any part of the line to the public with atmospheric apparatus because of delay in the construction and completion of the engines. The difficulties had been made greater by their having to use locomotives while the apparatus was being installed. On 1 September 1847 it was resolved not to incur expenditure on the system west of Totnes and to limit the expenditure already contracted for, until working between Exeter and Totnes had been fairly tried, except to provide assistant power up the eastern and western approaches to Dainton Summit, including a short section at 1 in 36.

On 13 September 1847 atmospheric working began

between Exeter and Teignmouth. Passengers approved of the smoothness of motion and absence of smoke and dust. Brunel was able to show that time lost on the locomotive part of the journey was made up on the atmospheric section. But there were breakages in essential parts, and the cupped leathers of the travelling-piston, which made it airtight, were often destroyed while it passed the inlet and outlet valves. Time and money were spent in an endeavour to overcome this. Water accumulated at times within the tube.

In the atmospheric tube the system of self-acting inlet and outlet valves, by which the piston was enabled to leave the tube on approaching a station and enter it again on recommencing its journey, were, on the whole, successfully adapted to their duty. The speed of the trains corresponded fully with the degree of vacuum obtained. After experiment, a form of air-pump valve was adopted which consisted of a number of long, delicate blades of spring steel, arranged in parallel. They rested on a series of true-faced bars, which crossed the end of the air passage. The slightest pressure outwards lifted the springs, and as the area of opening was large, a free passage was given to the air. On the current ceasing, the blades instantly replaced themselves in contact with the bars, clipping them tightly under a small reverse pressure and closing the passage.

To start a train rapidly from a station a short auxiliary vacuum tube was devised containing a piston which could be connected with the train by towrope, and thus draw it along until the piston of the piston car entered the main tube.

Serious and unexpected causes of failure developed in the longitudinal valve, leading to excessive leakage. When, because of leakage, the amount of air to be exhausted from the tube before the entry of a train was greatly increased, the operation had to begin much earlier. There was thus a longer time for leakage to occur and still more air to be pumped out. Therefore, a large increase of leakage involved a waste of power in an enormously increased proportion. As the electric telegraph had not been brought into full working order, warning that a train was late was not received at the engine houses. Pumping engines had then to be kept working needlessly long pumping out the air, which all the while was leaking in through the deteriorated valve.

Chiefly because of the defective valve the engines expended nearly three times the power they should have done for a given tractive duty, basing calculations on results of the Dalkey line. The cost of traction was nearly nine times as much as calculated, and between $2\frac{1}{2}$ and 3 times what it would have been with locomotive power.

If the valve had been efficient other defects might have been set right in time. It failed, partly because of the composition used to seal the joint where it opened, partly because of the material of which the valve consisted. Lime soap was eventually used for the composition, but its surface, exposed to light and air, formed a hard skin and a compound of soap and cod-oil had to be laid on to keep it soft. This required frequent renewal as it was apt to be drawn into the tube by the rush of air when the valve was opened. All this and repairs caused much expense.

It had not been anticipated how readily, with air pressure on one side and a partial vacuum on the other, the oily matters with which the leather of the valve was charged would escape from it. When the leather was saturated with water, the valve was tight, but frost supervening froze the water and made the leather stiff and unable to close properly. Drought made the leather intractable. Application of seal oil was the remedy but often it could not be applied quickly enough to prevent tearing. Moreover, both on the South Devon and the Croydon lines, rats quickly formed a taste for it.

In addition, the oxide, established in the iron plates of the valve by continued contact with damp leather, had been steadily absorbing the tannin. Thus the leather had become converted into comparatively decomposed tissue. In July 1848 Brunel discovered the condition of the valve and realised that the whole valve would have to be renewed from Exeter to Newton. He reported on 19 August 1848 to a committee of the Board appointed to examine the question. He showed that the engines had not so far worked very economically, but the valve was the cause of their chief difficulties. Much of it had been replaced after first cracking and then tearing in dry weather, but all of it was more or less defective from this cause. At parts which had given way the texture of the leather appeared to have been destroyed and had evidently been acted on by the iron. Brunel said that Samuda, who was liable for repair of the valve, alleged that the valve had deteriorated through having been exposed to damp. By painting, or, better, zincing or galvanising the iron plates and making them overlap a short distance, both the chemical and mechanical action of the plates on the leather appeared to be prevented.

Working expenses, said Brunel, would be much reduced by restoration of the valve and by further expenditure on improvement of the engines. Unless the patentees undertook the first and much extended the period during which they would maintain the valve in repair and offer some guarantee for its efficiency, the company was not justified in taking that on itself, or in incurring expense on engines.

The directors, while prepared to afford the patentees facilities for continuing their experiments, concluded that it was expedient to suspend the use of the system until it was made efficient at the expense of Samuda and the patentees. The proprietors concurred, and the line was worked by locomotives on and from 10 September 1848, only eight months exactly since the atmospheric working had been extended to Newton.

Thus ended what Devon people called the "Atmospheric Caper". From the time of the abandonment of the system, Brunel, again characteristically, declined any remuneration for his professional services as engineer to the South Devon beyond his nominal retaining fee. The experiment had cost £426,368, of which only some £50,000 was recovered from the sale of plant.

The engine houses were as striking as those on the Croydon line but in an Italianate style with the large chimney disguised as a campanile. Eleven were built, but the last three were never used: Exeter, Countess Weir, Turf, Starcross, Dawlish, Teignmouth, Bishopsteignton, Newton, Dainton, Totnes, Torquay branch. That at Starcross became a chapel.

As on the Croydon line, some good results had been obtained when the system was working well. The highest speed recorded on the South Devon was 68 m.p.h. with a 28-ton train, and an average speed was attained of 64 m.p.h. over four level miles.

On 14 August 1847, a month before the Exeter-Teignmouth service began, atmospheric traction was inaugurated on the Bois du Vésinet–Saint-Germain section (1 mile 646 yd.) of the Paris–Saint-Germain Railway. It had been recommended by M. Mollet, who had inspected the Dalkey line. This short section lasted until 20 July 1860.

A little later, Turettini laid down a 10-in. tube between Geneva and Plainpalais. Instead of a vacuum he used air pressure at the back of the piston—six times the atmospheric pressure. Air was taken from a reservoir into which the greater part was returned by the following downward train, thus doing away with brakes. A piston was connected with a two-wheel axle carrying a manometer and running on two small rails fixed into the tube itself. This axle pulled the locomotive and train by a stout iron chain. The air inside the tube and in front of the piston was at the pressure of the outside air. Only when the piston had passed was there need for the slit to be properly closed. The valve was a long bar of I-section, whose upper part rested on the tube before the piston arrived. The beam linking the piston with the upper truck was hollow and narrower at the same level as the slit than it was above and below it. In travelling, the front portion of the piston raised the I-valve a little, and the vertical, narrow portion of this valve had sufficient space inside the narrowed portion of the piston. The back of the piston pushed the I-valve higher, bringing its horizontal underpart against the inner surface of the slit, where it was kept by the pressure of the air at the back of the piston.

In 1845 a demonstration was held at a sawmills in York Road, Waterloo, of an atmospheric railway devised by Christopher Nickels. An airtight chamber or cast-iron pipe was laid below ground, and contained air compressed into one-third of the volume under ordinary atmospheric pressure by force pumps. Midway between the rails, square beams of wood or iron, 20-30 ft. long, were laid at intervals longitudinally and standing above the surface. The two vertical sides of the beam were slightly hollowed and along these superficial channels on each side were laid down tubes of gutta percha—then recently introduced from Singapore—leather, and canvas. These tubes communicated by intermediate pipes, fitted with stop cocks, with a compressed air reservoir. A skate-like arrangement, attached to the under part of the carriage, was so constructed as to act on the valves. Depression of a valve into the air cylinder released air which then passed into the tubes. On the underside of the car to be propelled were two solid rotating drums, one on each side of the rail, fixed on vertical spindles, which ran in supporting collars. These drums were so placed that when the car, which was supported on wheels running on rails in the ordinary way, passed over the horizontal beams, they embraced the two vertical sides and closely compressed the lateral elastic tubes so as to leave no air passage beyond the point of contact.

Some of the compressed air from a reservoir was admitted into the two tubes by the means already indicated, and, meeting resistance on the line of compression of the two drums, drove them, and consequently the carriage also, forward, following them with the same propulsive energy to the other extremity of the beam. Sufficient momentum was thus acquired to carry the car over the next length of beam, where the impulse was renewed, and so on along the line. The tubes were fitted in lengths of 50 yd., with a space between each, along both sides of the central rail or beam. Each length had one valve fitted to the top of the rail in question. The end of each length of tube farthest from the valve was left open for discharge of air after the passage of the drums, when they collapsed and were then ready for re-inflation when the next train came along. The "driver" in front controlled the apparatus at will.

Spectators at the demonstration expressed unanimous satisfaction. The compressed air, at 40 lb. p.s.i., admitted through a 1½-in. pipe, propelled the car rapidly. The advantages which Nickels claimed were perfect command of speed, greater facility of stopping, and less oscillation and vibration. Steep gradients were possible. There was no leakage beyond the amount needed for working.

In 1839 Nickels had patented another atmospheric railway, with a central rail and pneumatic tyre. The train ran on wheels in the usual way but the leading (hauling) carriage was narrower and differently built. Beneath it was a single wheel running on the centre rail. Rails, clear of the ground, were fitted on each side of the centre rail to guide the ordinary wheels of the carriages and prevent the central wheel from being lifted off by the inflation of the tube beneath it. The flexible tube was fitted to the top of the middle beam, and the periphery of the wheel ran over it. It was suggested that water instead of air might be used, and that, as the trains would vary in weight, two or more flexible tubes, side by side (affixed to the central beam), should be used, and one axle could carry as many wheels as there were tubes. Thus for a light train one tube only need be inflated. As an alternative, Nickels proposed a central wheel broad enough to be acted on by the whole of the tubes.

In a system devised by Pilbrow a piston running in a tube concealed beneath the railway imparted power to revolving spindles laid at intervals between the lines and engaging with a guide under the carriages. Brake pressure exerted on a small wheel attached to the spindles at intervals allowed air to escape from the underground tube and so halt the train.

The ideas of Vallance and Medhurst for an airtight tube were revived by T. W. Rammell, who in August 1864 opened an experimental line nearly 600 yd. long in the Crystal Palace grounds. A brick tunnel was built just large enough to admit a full-size coach, which had doors at the end and could carry some 35 passengers. It was encircled by a disc with a fringe of bristles which closely fitted the tunnel and obstructed the flow of air.

When the car was to make the down journey the brakes were released and it ran into the tunnel mouth, into which were fixed two airtight doors. These doors then closed on the carriage and air, forced into the tunnel by a 22-ft. dia. fan, pushed the car to the other end. The fan was then reversed, exhausting air from the tunnel and allowing the car to return. As it reached the upper end, the doors opened to allow it to emerge; its momentum carried it into the station where it was braked to a stop. The line, which included a 1 in 15 gradient and an 8 chain curve, was traversed in 50 seconds. The fare was 6d.

In the meantime Rammell had been the engineer to a similar venture which began in 1861, when the Pneumatic Despatch Company laid an experimental line, two-thirds of a mile long, in Battersea Park. A small carrier ran on rails in a 2 ft. 6 in. tube, from which a fan exhausted the air. The tube was transferred from Battersea and relaid between the North Western District Post Office in Eversholt Street and Euston Station, and began to carry mail in February 1863. The company then projected a 4 ft. 6 in. dia. tube from Euston to the General Post Office, of which the first section, to No. 245, Holborn, was opened in November 1865.

The following description of a visit to the Holborn station appeared in *The Illustrated London News* of 18 November 1865:—

"Emerging from the level of the street, the visitor passes along a corridor through a doorway, and emerges upon a gallery of considerable size, from which he looks down on a brick floor, supporting lines of rails, much as he might do from a railway platform down on to the line, but from a greater elevation. Underneath the corridor by which he has just entered he sees some mechanical appliances, suggestive partly

of an engine room and partly of a pointsman's gallery
outside a railway station; and below the level, again, on
which the white-jacketed engineer in charge is standing,
and supporting the platform on which both he and
these mechanical appliances rest, are a couple of open-
ings looking like black, polished modern chimney-
pieces, with the grates withdrawn.   These are the
mouths of the pneumatic tubes, of which one communicates with the North Western Railway; the other,
idle at present, will soon be drawing in and delivering
mail-bags from and to the postal headquarters in
London. The mouth of each tube is shut, when the tube
is exhausted of air, by iron folding doors, which meet,
not evenly, but at an angle projecting outwards so as to
resist the atmospheric pressure from without.   These
doors are made to fly open on the approach of a train,
the bolt which closes them being withdrawn by the
action of a spring lever, which underlies the rails, and
gives way beneath the weight of the train.   The carriages are shaped like a capital D turned over on its
straight side and mounted upon wheels.   Each end of
the carriage has a raised hood, or flange, shaped so as
to correspond with the interior of the tube, the dimensions of which are 4 ft. in height by 4 ft. 6 in. in
width.   The ordinary freight is expected to be in the
first instance letter bags, then probably railway parcels,
certain descriptions of market produce, and ultimately,
it may be, general merchandise.

"On the opening day the Duke of Buckingham,
Chairman of the Pneumatic Despatch Company, had
invited a number of scientific gentlemen to inspect the
apparatus.   After the train had made some successful
passages to and fro, several of the party expressed a
desire to pass through the tube themselves.   They were
warned that the line was 'not constructed with a view to
passenger traffic', and that they might find the way 'a

little rough'. The spirit of adventure, however, prompted them to take this strange journey, and each of the wagons had soon as many occupants as it could comfortably accommodate in the recumbent posture enforced by circumstances. Tarpaulin coverings were obtained for one or two of the carriages, but the greater number of the excursionists had to fit themselves in as best they could among the bags of shingle, which made up the temporary loading, taking care to keep their heads well below the edge of the carriages.

"The sensation at starting, and still more so upon arriving, (say some of the passengers) was not agreeable. For about a quarter-of-a-minute in each case there was a pressure upon the ears suggestive of a diving-bell experience, a suction like that with which one is drawn under a wave, and a cold draught of wind upon the eyes, having almost the effect of falling water; but once fairly within the tube, these sensations were got rid of, or left behind, and the motion had little more positive discomfort about it than would be attendant on riding on a 'lorry' over the worst ballasted line in England. The air within the tube was by no means foul or disagreeable; here and there a strong flavour of rust was encountered, but this was explained by the fact that, as the tube had to be laid in lengths, through various soils, and encountered in the process a large share of unfavourable weather, the corrosion on the surface of the iron could not be expected wholly to disappear until cleared away by the friction of constantly passing and repassing trains. On the arrival of the excursionists at the upper or Euston Square extremity of the line, they quitted their places for a few moments to inspect the smaller tube, which communicates with the Eversholt-street district post office, and then returned by the way they had come to Holborn.

"No doubt remained on the mind of any person who

Early view of the Lynmouth-Lynton cliff railway.

Bridgnorth Castle Hill Railway.

Montmartre Funicular, Paris.

Cliff railway at Southend - on - Sea.

oto: Régie Autonome des Transports Parisiens)

(Photo: courtesy of Southend Corporatio

(*Above*)   Engine house and station on New Cross-Croydon atmospheric line.

(*Below*)   Section of pipe of Croydon atmospheric line.

witnessed the opening trip as to the facilities which the system, if a sufficient number of stations can be incorporated with it, is calculated to afford, not only to the postal service but to the requirements of the general public. The scheme of the company, who, it seems, possess under their Act powers to lay down pneumatic tubes at any points within the jurisdiction of the Metropolitan Board of Works, is to construct similar lines to that now opened between the ten district post offices and the General Post Office, and between the different railway termini and goods depots in London, connecting with these lines the six principal London markets and other important points. For these purposes it is calculated that some thirty-five miles of tubing and a capital of £1,250,000 will be required, the cost per mile roughly estimated being from £30,000 to £35,000. The expenditure of the company hitherto has been probably £150,000 which would be largely in excess of this supposed average; but the sum mentioned includes the cost of preliminary experiments and also of seeking for two Acts of Parliament. The company expects that great profits will eventually accrue to them from the carriage of goods."

These sanguine hopes were unfulfilled, even after the opening of the St. Martins-le-Grand extension, and the whole enterprise was subsequently abandoned. As well as its lack of commercial success the line met technical troubles, of which the most persistent was leakage of air past the carrier. Much of the tube was filled in, but some is now used to carry telephone cables.

The first underground line in the United States was pneumatically operated. It was begun in 1869 by the Beach Pneumatic Transit Company, Alfred Ely Beach being the inventor of the system. The section built was 312 ft. long, under Broadway, New York, from Warren Street to just beyond Murray Street. The single tunnel,

driven by a shield, invented by Beach, was 9 ft. in diameter. This was the first use of the shield in America.
Although only twin 4 ft. 6 in. tunnels had been sanctioned, the company ingeniously argued that it had built
one large tunnel to carry the two smaller tubes, and,
having done so, it wanted to test whether passengers
could be carried pneumatically. (The authority covered
only the conveyance of goods.)

The line was opened on 26 February 1870, and
worked experimentally for a few months. The company
unsuccessfully sought further powers for pneumatic
lines, although authorised to build a steam underground, a venture prevented by lack of capital. When
the present subway line was being built under Broadway in 1912 part of the old pneumatic car and the rails
and shield came to light.

CHAPTER SIX

GUIDE RAIL SYSTEMS

IN the early days of railways inventors were much exercised over the need for greater safety combined with a reduction in constructional costs and train weights, a lessening of friction, and more freedom in traversing sharp curves.

In 1838 Colman exhibited his Patent Railway in Carlisle Street, Soho. The track consisted of iron plates on longitudinal timbers. The wheels ran freely on the axles. The main beam of the carriage was fastened by vertical bolts or pins to the front and rear axles, the axles turning horizontally round the pins. Perpendicularly to each axle was fixed a strong arm about half the length of the axle or more, and projecting from the centre of the carriage. Beneath each arm on four vertical axles were fixed four horizontal guide wheels, two under the axle and two towards the further end of the arm. Each pair of guides bore against the opposite side of a vertical iron plate laid in the centre of the railway. The bar of the axle was thus kept in the direction of, and the axle itself at right angles to, the centre line of road. Hence, each pair of carrying wheels was always moving parallel to the road, revolving on the axle without having any additional friction except that of the guide wheels.

On the outside of the carrying wheels of the engine was cast a projecting rim, roughened and smaller in diameter. When the engine began to ascend an incline this rim came upon a rail raised on the outside of the running rails just enough to lift the carrying wheels from those rails. The smaller circumference then run on and the roughened surface were thought to increase adhesion.

Kollman (not the same inventor as the Colman already mentioned) devised a method in which the wheels merely rested on the running rails. Horizontal guide wheels bore on the inside of the running rails and under the flange of a centre rail. It was advertised in 1845 by Kollman's Railway Locomotive & Carriage Improvement Company. A Major Parlby, formerly of the Indian Army, proposed to increase comfort and safety by fitting a semi-circular bumper at the ends of carriage frames with springs running over the axles. If this bumper were lifted by an obstruction the effect was to press the wheels more firmly on to the rails. As in Kollman's system the carrying wheels would merely rest on the rails, but these rails would be flanged and horizontal guide wheels would run under the flanges. This arrangement would enable coaches to be low-slung. The rounded ends of the coaches would contain the luggage then normally placed on the roof.

In the early 1840s William Prosser advocated the substitution of squared wooden rails of 8-in. scantling, let into wooden sleepers, for the expensive and unsatisfactory iron rails then in use. The iron rails of a mile of double line (72 lb. to yd.) then cost £3,000; the same length laid with 5,280 cu. ft. of beechwood would cost only £460, to which had to be added the expense of "paynizing" of the wood, at £70 per mile. Labour for laying the rails on Prosser's system cost £100, against £150 for the iron rails. On each system the sleepers cost £616 a mile, so that the saving in the cost of the permanent way was claimed to be £2,520 for a double mile of line, if Prosser's plan were adopted. "Paynizing" consisted of exhausting the air from the pores of the wood and forcing into it a solution of oxide of iron and lime; this was claimed to semi-petrify the wood, enabling it to resist the pressure of the wheels passing over it. The fact of the driving wheels of the engine having a better bite on the wood than on iron was thought to confer an additional advantage in taking a train of carriages up an incline.

Prosser proposed to dispense with flanges on the carrying wheels and use guide wheels fixed at an angle of 45 deg. and deeply grooved to engage with the upper surface and inner edge of the wooden rails.

In 1843 a Bill was deposited for a six-mile line from the London & South Western Railway at Woking to Guildford, to be worked on the Prosser system, at an estimated cost of £55,000.

Parliament sanctioned the scheme, and by the end of June 1844 72 of the 87 acres required for the line had been purchased, at an average price of £80 per acre. The total estimate for the land was £10,000 and £30,000 was allocated for the construction, but the contract was let for £23,257. Prosser stated at the company meeting, when these figures were mentioned, that the average cost of an iron railway was £25,000 a mile.

It was intended to extend the line through Godalming and Haslemere, to the South Coast, but in the autumn of 1844 it was proposed to construct an atmospheric railway from Epsom through the same district to Portsmouth. This threatened incursion into the district claimed by the London & South Western Railway as its preserve so frightened it that it sought to purchase the Guildford Junction Railway to enable it better to fight the atmospheric project.

As the change from iron to wooden rails would be inconvenient on a through route, the L.S.W.R. agreed in December 1844 to purchase the Guildford Junction Railway for £75,000, the railway to be completed as a single line with iron rails. Of this amount £20,000 was paid to Prosser as compensation for not using his system, but as the construction of the six miles of single line cost much less than the £55,000 paid by the L.S.W.R., the Guildford Junction shareholders also made a good bargain.

To test Prosser's system, the leading wheels were removed from a locomotive and an experimental line, 174 yd. long, was laid down near Vauxhall Bridge. The gradients were 1 in 95, 1 in 22, and 1 in 9 and a curve of 720 ft. radius was included. Speed was limited by the short run, but the power given to the engine by the bite of the wheels on the wood enabled the train to get up to 24 m.p.h. and stop in a distance of 24 yd. In the presence of several engineers, a carriage laden with passengers ascended an incline of 1 in 9, the rails being in a very bad state at the time because of damp. The curve was at the centre of the line and thus had to be taken at maximum speed, thoroughly testing the safety of the bevel wheels.

The engine used in experiments weighed some 6 tons and in two months of trials passed over the track 28,000 times—equivalent to nearly seven years' traffic at 12 engines a day. The rails consisted of Scotch fir, about 9 ft. long and 6 in. square. After the trials they showed no sign of wear on the upper surface; the saw marks were not even erased and the bevel wheels had not impaired the edges.

Guide or "anti-friction" wheels were placed two in front and two behind the driving wheels, on axles, at an angle of 45 deg. A deep groove formed by two flanges was made in their circumference, exactly corresponding to the inner and upper angle of the rail, and they served as the guiding wheels to the whole machine.

When the railway was straight, only one of each pair of bevel wheels could be in action at the same time, according to the tendency of the carriage to move to one side or the other from the centre of the rail. On a curve, the outside bevel wheel of the front pair, and the inside one of the back pair, came into play, and counteracted the disposition of the carriage to fly off at a tangent with the curve. Springs had to be inserted between frame and body. If the frame had been sprung, the guide wheels would have left the rails at every bump.

In the summer of 1845 Prosser's Patent Railway Guide Wheel Company operated a railway to demonstrate the Prosser system on Wimbledon Common. It was about two miles in circumference, and included gradients of 1 in 50 and 1 in 120, and a 10 ch. curve. Part of the line was laid with iron and part with wooden rails.

To test the difference in power required to propel a carriage with the guide wheels and with the flange wheels, an experiment was made on the Hayle Railway in Cornwall. A laden wagon, fitted with guide wheels and with the flanges on the bearing wheels removed, was found to be propelled with one-fourth less power than a similar wagon carrying an equal load but with the flanges preserved. Prosser claimed that an engine weighing 10 tons, running on wood, had more tractive power than one weighing 18 tons running on iron, and that carriages built to weigh $1\frac{1}{2}$ tons would be as strong as those running on iron and weighing 3 tons.

A model locomotive and train, constructed to a scale of $1\frac{1}{2}$ in. to the foot, was built and travelled round a curve of 9 ft. radius at a speed equivalent to 40 m.p.h. and covered upwards of 50,000 miles without accident.

Prosser pointed out that the only obstacle to the use of guide wheels on ordinary lines was the usual form of the chairs, which came to within $1\frac{1}{2}$ in. of the top of the rail and left insufficient room for the groove of the guide wheel. He proposed that a chair with lower inner cheek should be used on new lines so that either flanged or guide wheels could be used.

Prosser later experimented with a system which added a third double-flanged wheel in the centre of the axle to run on a central rail. He assumed that three wooden rails would be cheaper than two metal ones and that a train with such a centre wheel could negotiate sharper curves than one with flanges on the carrying wheels.

Apart from the Guildford line, Prosser's ideas were not taken up at the time and he finally turned his attention to the atmospheric system of propulsion.

While Prosser was perfecting his system in England, Arnoux, the works manager of a French road transport undertaking, Messageries Laffitte, proposed a line to be built to a system tried out by him at Saint-Mande. It aimed at reducing constructional costs to the minimum by permitting curves up to 30-m. radius and rolling stock so built that the axles would follow a true curve. A commission presided over by Arago reported favourably on it, and a line on Arnoux's system from Paris to Sceaux was authorised on 5 August 1844 and opened on 23 June 1846 by one of King Louis-Philippe's sons.

It began from the Barrière d'Enfer (now Denfert-Rochereau), where there was a 25-m. radius terminal loop. As far as Bourg-la-Reine there were no excessive curves but thence to Sceaux the line was laid out deliberately with a succession of curves to display the advantages claimed for the system. For a distance of 600 m. in a straight line the line took 2,600 m., with reverse curves of 50 m. At the Sceaux terminus there was another loop. The gauge was 1·75 m.

The railway was popular and in 1854 was extended 16 km. from Bourg-la-Reine to Orsay. In 1857 it was amalgamated with the new Paris–Orleans Railway,

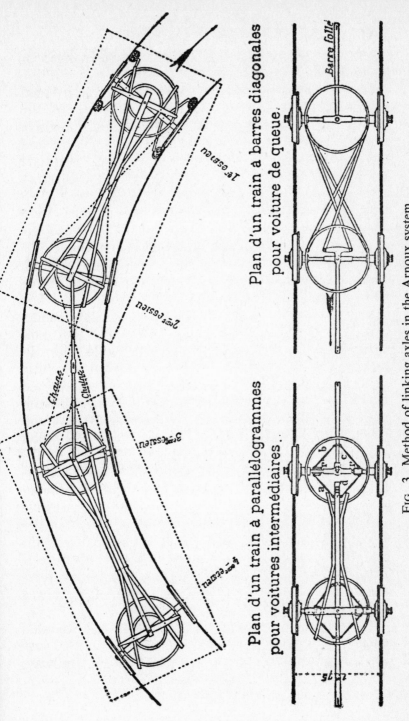

Plan d'un train à barres diagonales
pour voiture de queue.

Barre folle

Plan d'un train à parallélogrammes
pour voitures intermédiaires.

Fig. 3. Method of linking axles in the Arnoux system

which extended it again, to Limours, in 1867. Both extensions had curves of no more than normal severity. Although the system worked well, the isolation of the line led the Paris–Orleans to decide in 1883 to adopt normal working, ease the severe curves, and convert to standard gauge. The conversion was completed in 1893, and the line was extended at the city end to the Luxembourg. In 1932 the Sceaux line (Luxembourg–Massy Palaiseau, and Bourg-la-Reine–Sceaux Robinson) was electrified and transferred to the Paris Metropolitan.

In Arnoux's system the locomotives were like those of Prosser with flangeless carrying wheels resting on the running rails and inclined guide wheels pressing obliquely against the top inner rail surface. The trains were articulated. The carriages had flanged wheels, running free on their axle ends. Each axle was pierced in the centre by a pin about which it could turn. As the accompanying drawing shows, the two axles of a coach were linked by compensating beams. There were no buffers and the coaches were linked by a single rigid bar, as the distance between axles had to remain constant. This caused rough starts and complicated shunting. The first locomotives were of the 2-2-2 tender type. Later engines built by the Paris–Orleans were of the same wheel arrangement and there were also 2-4-2 tanks.

The Oreti Railway in the extreme south of South Island, New Zealand, was laid to a system resembling Prosser's. To reduce the cost of construction, wooden rails were used, and the locomotives and rolling stock were built with flangeless carrying wheels and inclined guide wheels. The railway was opened on 18 October 1864, between Invercargill and Makarewa, as the first section of a planned route to Winton, 19 miles from Invercargill, and eventually the goldfields of Wakatipu.

But the wooden rails soon decayed, warped, or became spongy, and the four locomotives, supplied from Australia, were found to be unsuitable. By early 1867 traffic had ceased and the line lay derelict for a time until relaid with iron rails and extended.

Larmanjat's system was tried near Mulhouse in 1869 on a three-mile section with 20-ft. curves and 1 in 13 gradients. A traction engine with two driving wheels running on the road as usual had a leading wheel with two flanges running on a single tram rail, nearly buried in the centre of the road. The cars or wagons had a front and rear wheel running on the rail, and a middle pair of small road wheels. The object was to give to most of the train the advantage of the greatly reduced friction on the rail, while the engine could use all the adhesion available from the road.

In the system of Saint-Pierre and Goudal the locomotive was intended to run on a special track, composed of a single centre rail, and two asphalt strips on which ran four wheels with broad tread. Two pairs of wheels placed almost horizontally under the locomotive gripped the centre rail rather as in the Fell system.

The Larmanjat system, or one closely similar, was adopted by the Lisbon Steam Tramways Co. Ltd., which proposed to operate two detached routes, one from Lisbon to Torres Vedras, about 33 miles, the other from Lisbon along the coast to Cascaes and thence inland to Pero Pinheiro, 28 miles. Permission could not be obtained to construct a line through the city linking the termini, and it seems doubtful whether any services were operated, as the company failed about a year after construction was begun. Sharp Stewart & Co. Ltd., of Manchester, built for the company a locomotive of which the wheel arrangement when viewed in elevation was 4-2-4. In fact there were single driving wheels, of

3 ft. 9 in. dia., flangeless and with 14 in. treads for running on the road surface. The leading and trailing bogies were centrally placed and each had two 1 ft. 9 in. dia. wheels in tandem; their tyres had centre grooves instead of the ordinary treads and flanges and ran on a centre rail. Chains at the leading and trailing ends allowed the bogies to swivel up to 18 deg. to negotiate sharp curves.

The so-called Superficial Railway of Köstlin was tried out in 1873 at the Mödling Works, near Vienna. Between the rails were fixed two (or, on a narrow-gauge line, one) longitudinal timber sleepers. Each sleeper was divided into three parallel strips, the centre one of oak, with the end of the grain upwards, and projecting a little above those at the sides. It thus formed a wooden rail, on which bore a wide wheel fastened to the driving-axle of the engine. This wide wheel was of such diameter as just to lift the ordinary wheels of the engine off the rails, without bringing their flanges above rail level; but for greater safety it was itself provided with flanges. The vehicles ran on the rails, as usual. This arrangement, like Larmanjat's, gave great adhesion to the engine, while retaining the iron track for the train. The engine was a six-coupled tank.

A Major F. Dutton, Superintendent of Motor Transport in South Africa, invented a road-rail system in which a tractor was designed to use both the low tractive resistance of rail vehicles and the high tractive effort of solid rubber tyres on roads. The driving wheels of the tractor ran on a concrete or macadam road, but the load was carried in vehicles running on light rails. Gradients of 1 in 12 and 30-ft. curves could be negotiated.

The tractors followed road lorry practice and in many instances could be arranged for ordinary road traction by raising the special bogie used for guiding when hauling a railborne load. The carrying wheels of the tractor, that is, those which merely carried the part of its total weight not supported on the driving wheels, ran on the rails, which thus automatically guided the machine and pivoted the driving wheels on the prepared wheel-ways.

The first Dutton line was laid down at Canada Junction, near Johannesburg, with gradients and curves made particularly severe to afford a thorough test. Sir William Hoy, then the General Manager of the South African Railways, said that "its inventor has not yet succeeded in converting the technical advisers of the Administration to accept all that is claimed for it, but I am of opinion that the principle of the system is sound and desire to see it tried in a suitable district for the actual conveyance of public traffic".

Major Dutton subsequently joined forces with General Stronach to exploit the invention commercially and Roadrail Loco-Tractors Limited was formed. At the British Empire Exhibition at Wembley a double-track Stronach-Dutton line, with end loops, was laid down and carried visitors.

The rail gauge was 2 ft. and the driving wheel track was 5 ft. 6 in. between centres. There were four petrol tractors, each of four cylinders. Each had 4-ft. dia. rear road wheels and front road wheels of 3-ft. diameter. In addition there were two Sentinel steam tractors with two rail bogies and only one pair of road wheels. Covered coaches with sides open above the waist line were used.

In 1950 the Paris Transport Authority began to consider the application of the rubber tyre to underground rolling stock. In view of loading restrictions the use of a multi-axle bogie as had been tried by the French National Railways (see Chapter Seven) was not possible, and the Authority therefore harked back to the idea of a guide. The emergence of the heavy-duty road tyre able to bear a load of 4 *tonnes* on a wheel of a diameter less than 1 m. aided this solution.

A new form of guidage was developed using both horizontal guide wheels and a flanged wheel running above the ordinary rails in normal service. These wheels come into contact with the rail only when a rubber carrying tyre deflates or the vehicle has to move from one track to another. Trials began in 1952 on the disused Porte de Lilas–Pré Saint-Gervais section of the Paris Metropolitan of a coach fitted with pneumatic-tyred wheels outside flanged wheels. The pneumatic-tyred wheels ran on timber longitudinals laid outside rails. The flanged wheels were normally clear of the steel rails, coming into contact with them only if a tyre deflated or when the car was shunted. In front of and behind each bogie were horizontal pneumatic-tyred wheels which pressed against the underside of flat-bottom rails laid on their sides.

The success of its experiments prompted the Authority to place orders for new four-car trains of similar design, to run on its line No. 11, from Châtelet to Mairie des Lilas, which has been adapted for their use. The undertaking hopes that the greater adhesion of the rubber tyre will permit more rapid acceleration and deceleration and thus decrease the interval between trains. Ultimately the whole Paris system may be so converted and it is proposed to apply the principle to a projected underground railway in Istanbul.

In our own day some of the basic ideas of Prosser and his contemporaries have been revived, with varying success. The modern applications have depended on the use of pneumatic tyres, corresponding to the flangeless carrying wheels of the early systems, and inclined or horizontal guide wheels. E. C. Noble, who had been Chief Mechanical Engineer of the Entre Rios Railway, Argentina, devised a light, inclined guide wheel on a detachable bracket to be fitted to commercial road vehicles to enable them to run with their rubber-tyred road wheels on rail. He then designed a lightweight rubber-tyred bogie railcar, fitted with six steel guide wheels on fixed brackets and bearing at an angle on the rail. A vehicle of this type for the Entre Rios Railway was tried between Bletchley and Oxford in 1935.

Ing. Alejandro Goicochea Omar, the Spanish engineer and inventor of the lightweight Talgo train, has developed an interesting elevated guide-rail system which is being tried out in Spain and Argentina. In this the track consists of prefabricated reinforced-concrete beams, supported 1 m. above ground level. On the top surface run the pneumatic tyres of the train. Two solid rubber guide rollers bear obliquely against the inside of the beams. The wheels are so placed that the vehicle, of light weight, runs partly between the rails, so that the centre of gravity is low. An air-screw provides the motive power. As the coaches are only 2 m. long, the train resembles a flexible tube. A commercial speed of 200 km.p.h. is envisaged.

CHAPTER SEVEN

PNEUMATIC TYRE SYSTEMS

IN February 1929, André Michelin, of the famous tyre company, wrote to his brother Edouard that the noise of the train wheels had made it impossible for him to sleep while on a journey to the Riviera. This set Edouard thinking about the possibility of using pneumatic tyres on railway lines. So vigorously did he take up the idea that tests were started about the middle of 1929 and in October of that year a 40-h.p. car began running on the feeder line to the Michelin factory at Clermont-Ferrand. In the winter of 1929-30 tests continued on the Laqueuille–Le Mont-Dore line. Despite the gradients and curves of the line a speed of nearly 50 m.p.h. was attained. Early the following summer tests went on on the Saint-Florent–Issoudun line, and on 26 January 1931 an 18-seat vehicle was put in service on that route.

New prototypes followed each other in quick succession. No. 5, consisting of a duralumin fuselage, rather like that of an aeroplane, which was carried at the front by a Hispano-Suiza 46-h.p. automobile chassis and on a bissel truck at the rear, had 10 seats. No. 9, used on the route from Saint-Arnoult-en-Yveline to Coltainville (on the Paris–Chartres line) had 12 seats and a Hispano-Suiza 95-h.p. petrol motor of the type used for road vehicles. On 10 September 1931 this car ran direct from Paris to Deauville, 137 miles, in 123 minutes, an average of $66\frac{1}{2}$ m.p.h.

This car was followed by the 1931-type "Micheline"

PROSSER'S NEW WOODEN GUIDE WHEEL RAILWAY.

PROSSER'S WOODEN RAILWAY, WIMBLEDON COMMON.

GUIDE WHEELS.—FRONT VIEW.

PORTION OF TRAM.

ENGINE, TENDER, AND CARRIAGE.—SIDE VIEW.

(*Photo: courtesy of British Railways*)

Prosser's Guide Wheel Railway on Wimbledon Common.

(*Above*)   Larmanjat single guide rail train.

(*Below*)   Paris Métro rubber tyre train.

(*Photo: Régie Autonome des Transports Parisiens*)

with 18 seats. This had a 95-h.p. Panhard motor. It had three axles at the front, two driven axles, and a bissel truck at the rear. In 1932, a new Micheline with 24 seats appeared. This was carried on two bogies; the front one had three axles, the two which drove the vehicle being coupled by a chain. The motor, a Panhard similar to that of the previous model, drove the centre axle. The rear carrying bogie had two axles only. Ten of these cars went into public service on the French railways. They ran from six in the morning to 10.30 at night and covered 530 km. daily.

The Michelines continued to grow. In January 1933 a car with 36 seats was shown publicly. This was Type 16, which was provided with a conning-tower for the driver giving him a good view of the track over the roof of the car, which could travel at full speed in either direction. This car had a Hispano-Suiza engine of 220 h.p. and could travel at more than 70 m.p.h. The light aluminium body—the car weighed only eight tons—and the adhesion of the rubber tyres, some four times that of steel wheels, enabled rapid starts to be made from rest. The braking performance has been described as "spectacular". Twenty-six of these cars were built in 1934-35.

In March 1934 the 56-seat car made its appearance. It had a 12-cylinder Hispano-Suiza motor with a four-speed gearbox. The motor drove, by mechanical transmission, the inner axles of one of the two eight-wheel bogies. This was Micheline Type 20. Types 21 and 22 followed with minor modifications only and with the same number of seats. Metre-gauge Michelines were put into service on African railways and also in Indo-China.

A 24-seat car was tried in England in 1932 on the Southern Railway between Ascot and Alton and also on the London Midland & Scottish Railway between Bletchley and Oxford. This car had ten wheels, arranged in a group of six beneath the bonnet and driving cab and a further group of four wheels at the rear. The pneumatic tyres had metal flanges beside them to perform the usual function of keeping the car to the rails. The tyres had a wooden hoop inside which prevented deflation to more than a small extent and ensured that a punctured tyre would not derail the coach. The car weighed about 5 tons and looked rather like a motor-coach on rails. At the same time, the Budd Company, in America, built a Michelin car under licence from the French firm and tried it out on several lines in the U.S.A. This car had a stainless steel body with 40 seats, and a 90-h.p. diesel motor with electric transmission, though the use of a 120-h.p. petrol motor with mechanical transmission was considered.

A Michelin type car was tested in England in 1935, with certain improvements, under the auspices of Armstrong-Siddeley Limited, of Coventry, by whom it was built. It was known as the Coventry Pneumatic Railcar, and was 54 ft. 3 in. in length and weighed 8 tons 5 cwt. light, or 13 tons 5 cwt. with a full load.

This car had two eight-wheel bogies and three axles of the front bogies were driven and connected by chains. Accounts state that the car carried 56 passengers, but drawings seen by the authors show seats for 46 only. This may be due to the provision of a luggage compartment, the space for which could, of course, be used for additional seating. The French cars used coiled steel compression rings and rubber, but semi-elliptic springs took their place in the Coventry model. The 275-h.p. Armstrong-Siddeley motor drove through a Wilson gearbox. On its first trial run the car achieved nearly 68 m.p.h. Although the car had a good reception, it was decided that traffic on British railways was too intensive to enable Michelines to be used on any but secondary lines. Despite the example of the French railways, they were never used even for this service.

On 14 December 1936, a 56-seat Micheline went to Czechoslovakia for display and was shown to railway officials in Prague between 14 December 1936 and 2 January 1937. On 6 January a new Micheline with 96 seats, Type 23, covered the 263 miles between Paris and Clermont-Ferrand in 4 hours, with seven intermediate stops. This car had a carrying bogie at each end and a motor bogie in the centre, driven by a 420-h.p. Panhard motor. The gearbox was of Cotal type with four speeds. Hydraulic transmission was used. Rubber was used extensively on these cars to form elastic joints. One of these cars was shown at the New York Exhibition in April 1939. Finally, Michelines in three sections appeared, with 106 seats, driven by two 250-h.p. Hispano-Suiza petrol motors. The prototype had run as early as 1 April 1936 on the line from Clermont-Ferrand through Brive to Tarbes, some 390 miles.

By the outbreak of the second world war there were 140 Michelines running in France and in the French colonies, but the war brought their running to an end. The cars aged, and diesel engines, too heavy for the Michelines, have proved more economical. Nevertheless, they were marvellously adapted to their time, and, as we shall see shortly, the rubber tyre on rails was by no means outmoded.

The Michelines were not alone in the field. On 26 March 1935 a car with Dunlop tyres, built by Etablissements Fouga, appeared. This weighed 17 tons and had seats for 49 passengers. There were two four-axle bogies, with the outside wheels of flanged railway type to act as guides and the inner wheels equipped with pneumatic tyres. There was a 150-h.p. diesel motor driving through mechanical transmission and a four-speed gearbox. The Noble car for the Entre Rios Rail-

way has been mentioned in a previous chapter. Trials
with a three-car set built by Daimler in Austria were
carried out on the Vienna–Semmering line from 1932.
This had steel wheels incorporating a pneumatic
cushion and known as the Daimler-Puch wheel.

The Michelin railway wheel had a steel flange to keep
it on the rails, but the load was carried by a pnuematic
tyre butting against the flange. The load which could be
carried by any one tyre was severely limited by the
narrow rail surfaces, which is why the Michelines had
so many wheels. Nevertheless, the load per tyre was
gradually increased from 1,430 lb. in 1932 to 2,650 lb. in
1937. This increase was due mainly to the introduction
of the *Métalic* tyre, which had a steel wire carcase.
Tyres in use after the war averaged 21,750 miles in
service.

Light construction was essential with these cars because of this tyre-loading factor. It was claimed, however, with some justice, that the Michelines gave good
running because the tyres absorbed any unevenness of
the track and, because of the cushion of air in the tyres,
gave smooth and silent riding. The adhesion factor, already mentioned, enabled the cars to start and stop
very quickly.

The Michelines were built on road motor principles,
but the idea of a stronger bogie, specially built for railway use, was considered in 1939. The investigations
continued during the German occupation and trials
were carried out in North Africa from 1942. At last a
sturdy five-axle bogie was produced capable of being
fitted to railway coaches and even to complete trains.
The axles are connected with the rigid frame through
flexible devices called "Bibax". The "Bibax" is essen-
tially a rubber block with strictly-determined flexibility.
The body of the carriage is carried on two transverse
springs of the bogie capable of moving in special slides

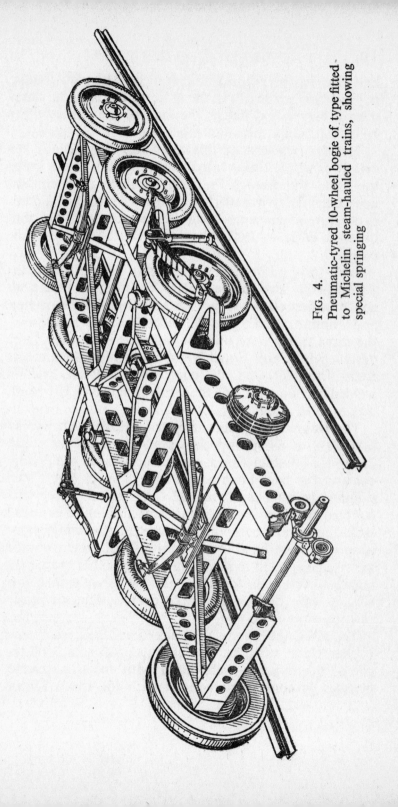

and also on two longitudinal springs. The whole bogie
is rigid enough to allow the train to continue to travel
even if a tyre is deflated, the load of the deflated tyre
being shared by the other nine.

The development of this ten-wheel bogie made the
design of whole trains fitted with pneumatic tyres possible, and the French National Railways, which had
now considerable experience with the Michelin rail-
cars, showed an immediate interest in the idea and
ordered, early in 1947, three trains fitted with the new
bogies.

Each train comprised a composite second class/bag-
gage coach, two second class coaches, a first class
coach, a first class coach with a section fitted as a bar,
and a dining car. To give the widest possible experience,
the three trains were built of different materials. One,
designed by Carel Fouché, was in stainless steel to the
Budd formula; one, designed by Chausson, was in
welded carbon steel; and the third, designed by C.I.M.T.,
was in light alloy.

The trains had certain similar features. All had 48
first class or 64 second class seats in each coach, and
250 in the complete train, excluding those in the dining-
car and the bar. Each coach was 76 ft. in length and
weighed 16 tons empty and 21 tons loaded. They were
coupled together by a central semi-automatic coupling
including rubber components. Special pneumatic shock
absorbers were fixed to the end-walls of the coach and
were large enough to press against each other even if the
coaches were considerably out of alignment. The
wheels were fitted with brake drums actuated by an
oleo-pneumatic system.

To meet the needs of track-circuiting, which the
rubber tyres, with their insulating properties, complicated, the coaches were fitted with metallic contact
brushes in continuous contact with the rail. Special

steps, which could be withdrawn to improve the stream-lining of the coach, gave access to the train. A patented gangway, incorporating rubber bellows, communicated between the coaches.

The three trains were required to go into traffic in 1948 to give an express service between Paris and Stras-bourg at an average speed of 62 m.p.h. In service, they were hauled by type 230K streamlined 4-6-0 steam locomotives.

Two rather similar coaches were ordered for trials by the Swiss Federal Railways. The second class coach was of aluminium alloy and the third class coach of mild steel. Had these met all requirements, it was in-tended to form complete rubber-tyred trains to be hauled by the "Re4/4" class electric locomotives of the S.F.R.

The Bugatti petrol-driven trains, which achieved speeds of more than 100 m.p.h. on the former Paris–Lyons–Mediterranean Railway in France, had wheels in which rubber pads were placed between wheel-centres and the steel rims, giving the effect of rubber tyres. A pneumatic-tyre rail omnibus used at one time on the Great Northern Railway of Ireland had rather similar wheels, except that the rubber "sandwich" was actually a pneumatic tyre.

The omnibus was a single-deck vehicle which, when converted in 1934, was already five years old. Little alteration was made to the vehicle as equipped for road running except that the steering mechanism was re-moved and the special wheels fitted. The equipment was designed by G. B. Howden, then Chief Engineer, and R. W. Meredith, Works Manager, of the G.N.R.(I).

The wheels were of normal road type but were dished to enable them to conform to the 5 ft. 3 in. gauge track. Wide-based Dunlop tyres were fitted with treads smooth except for two circumferential grooves. Outer steel rims were arranged to fit over the tyres and these rims were flanged like railway wheels. On the inner surface they were machined to the profile of the rubber tyres and had two ribs which fitted into the grooves in the tyres. As the outer rims were slightly smaller in diameter than the tyres, they fitted very tightly when the pneumatic tyres were fully inflated. Up to 30 November 1953, two buses equipped in this manner had run 1,445,730 miles without needing tyre replacements. Similar cars have operated on the Sligo, Leitrim & Northern Counties Railway.

Track circuiting needs again caused difficulty and eventually the special wheels were removed from the front axle and normal steel railway wheels substituted to meet the situation.

An interesting extension of the use of pneumatic tyres is in the various vehicles which have been and still are being built to run on road or rail alternately. In these there are usually two sets of wheels—flanged steel wheels for rail travel and pneumatic tyres for the road—with mechanism for bringing one set or the other into use.

In Britain, these vehicles are commonly known as "road-railers". One of the first was a Karrier 26-seat passenger coach built, after more than two years of experiments, for the London Midland & Scottish Railway. This complied with the regulations for road use and also met railway requirements for running on the railway track. It had a 37·2-h.p. engine of the type fitted to normal road passenger vehicles at the time. The gearbox gave a 7:1 ratio for use on the road and a 4·2:1 ratio for rail use. These were the top gears, of course, and they gave speeds of up to 60 m.p.h. on the road and 75 m.p.h. on rails. The vehicle weighed just over 7 tons. A feature of the running was that the 8 m.p.g. achieved on the road was doubled on the railway, probably because of the comparatively gentle gradients and the better gear ratio.

A road-rail lorry was built by the same firm for the London & North Eastern Railway. This had a 31–48 h.p. engine and was limited to about 30 m.p.h. on the road and a little more on the railway. The capacity of this type of lorry ranged from 30 cwt. to 8 tons in Britain, where it had to comply with the normal regulations for road vehicles, and up to 20 tons for use abroad.

Both passenger and goods vehicles used similar wheel-changing apparatus. The railway wheels were fitted, at the normal 4 ft. $8\frac{1}{2}$ in. gauge, to the axles of the vehicle. Outside these, the road wheels were mounted on eccentrics fitted to the end of the axle where it protruded through the rail wheel. A locking device enabled the road wheels to be fixed concentrically with the railway wheels. To change the wheels, the vehicle was driven on the road to any suitable point where the road surface was made up level with the rails. The vehicle was then driven along the railway until the road surface fell away and the weight came on the railway wheels. The driver then raised each road wheel by rotating it on its eccentric until it was above rail level and fastened it by a pin to the chassis, locking it in place. Only the rail wheels rotated when the vehicle was on the railway track, the drive being cut off from the road wheels by taking out pins which locked the two wheels together and which were also used to secure the road wheels in the raised position. Special supports for the road wheels when in this position folded into the body when the vehicle was in use on the road. There were certain complications connected with the process, most of which were taken care of automatically by the mechanism, but on the whole wheel-changing was a simple and quick matter.

The coach mentioned worked over the branch be-

tween Stratford-on-Avon and Blisworth, on the Euston–
Rugby main line. It picked up passengers at a Stratford
hotel, took them to the station, and was there converted
to a railway vehicle for the rest of the trip. The great
possibility was thought to lie in its use on those branch
lines where stations are some distance from the villages
they serve or in serving places beyond railheads. On the
whole, however, it seems to be accepted today that once
a vehicle is on the road it may as well complete its journey by that means. There are still obvious possibilities,
however, in countries where good roads are few and the
railway would serve conveniently for the trunk portion
of the run.

The lorry mentioned had buffers attached to the
chassis at front and rear and thus presented rather an
odd appearance on the road. It was used on the West
Highland line in Scotland for carrying men and materials for permanent way work. An improved form of
wheel-changing device was adopted which used a slotted
hub and had other advantages which enabled the wheels
of the vehicle to be changed in less than five minutes.

A coach on the road-rail principle, built by Karrier
Motors Limited, ran on the lines of the Rotterdam
Tramways in Holland.

In recent years there has been a number of experiments, some very successful, in giving vehicles change-
able wheels to enable them to be towed on road wheels
or run as normal rail vehicles. Particular progress has
been made in the U.S.A. and in Germany.

A combination road-rail car, in effect a Pontiac station wagon with railway guide wheels, has been introduced in the U.S.A. as an inspection vehicle. It is
known as the Fairmont Series A A34 inspection motor-
car. It has a 205-h.p. V-8 engine, and can seat eight persons on three cross-seats. There are all the usual motor-
car refinements including a heater and defroster, power

steering and brakes, a Dualoc power-dividing differential, and dual-range hydramatic transmission. Its unique feature is the provision of guide wheels for rail use which can be raised or lowered at will by small hydraulic cylinders, and are held in position by a separate mechanical lock. The hydraulic cylinders are fed from a combination electric motor and pump unit which has controls at both ends of the car. The normal steering can be locked for railway travel, an indicator on the dashboard showing when the lock is in use.

In France a 2½-ton Renault van has been adapted to run on road or rail. It is a catenary maintenance vehicle, and its dual nature has been adopted to reduce line occupation on the railway. The van can travel as near as possible to the point where it is required for work by road, run on to the track to work, and leave the railway again as soon as its work is finished. The vehicle is fitted with a turning plate which lifts it high enough from the ground for the wheels to be changed. When this operation is to be carried out, the van is driven to a position where it stands across the railway track which it is to use and is then lifted and the wheels changed. It is then swung round into position over the rails and lowered on to them. The operation takes under five minutes. When the van is travelling on the rails the steering is locked. Power for the lifting and turning movements is supplied from the van itself by hydraulic apparatus.

The process has been carried the whole way on one Swiss line where the track has been lifted and a bus with trailers has been formed into a "road-train" to perform the services.

The pneumatic-tyred trains on the Metro in Paris are described in Chapter Six.

CHAPTER EIGHT

MONORAILS

M OST people probably think of a true monorail line as a single track laid, like an ordinary railway, on the surface of the ground. The great difficulty with such a railway is in keeping the balance of the train. Most monorails, as will be seen elsewhere in this book, require auxiliary balancing rails or some form of pannier construction or overhead suspension to overcome this difficulty.

Nevertheless, true monorails have been invented and run experimentally. The most important of these systems, which depend on gyroscopes for the stability of the cars, was invented by an Irishman, Louis Brennan. Brennan was born at Castlebar, Co. Mayo, in 1852, and went to Australia as a boy, living in Melbourne until 1880. His first claim to fame was as the inventor of a torpedo which could be controlled by wires from the shore. This invention was adopted by the British Government in 1882 for harbour defence and Brennan was made Superintendent of the Government factory which turned out the torpedoes. This position he held from 1887 to 1896. He remained Consulting Engineer to the factory until 1907. His work with his torpedo resulted in his being made a C.B. in 1892.

Brennan's experiments with monorails began in 1896 and he applied for his first patent on 11 December 1903, and exhibited a large model of his car to the Royal Society on 8 May 1907. His full-size car was not publicly demonstrated, however, for some years and might not have been then had news not reached Brennan that similar ideas had been developed so vigorously in Germany that it was proposed to hold a public demonstration of a monorail car on the gyroscope principle, with a car 17 ft. in length, at the Zoological Gardens, in Berlin, on 10 November 1909.

Telegrams were hastily despatched to the Press inviting them to attend a demonstration of the Brennan car on the same day at Gillingham, Kent. Brennan was determined that Germany, which had adopted Brennan's own ideas, should not be the first in the field.

At Gillingham, Brennan had laid down a single rail track which included a circle an eighth of a mile in circumference and straight run of some 400 yd. When the car, 40 ft. long, emerged from its shed, an eye-witness said it "made an impression as of some uncanny monster . . . on its single row of bogie wheels, moved steadily over serpentine curves, merely leaning to one side or the other to maintain its balance, and took the circle, and then the straight, with as much stability of position as if it had been supported on two sets of rails".

The onlookers were allowed to travel on the platform which was built on the front part of the car. Forty persons at a time were carried round the track. As an experiment, on one run, the whole party on board moved to one side of the vehicle. Instead of that side sinking, as might have been expected, it rose slightly, the gyroscopes over-compensating for the increased load while they brought the car back to equilibrium. Brennan told the correspondents that two ton weights could be placed on the edge of the car with similar results. Just the same thing happened when the car went round a curve—it leaned to one side as a cyclist would do to preserve its balance.

This impressive, but hasty, demonstration was followed on 25 February 1910 by a much more elaborate performance which was attended by scientists, engineers, military officers, railway officers, and, among others, representatives of colonial governments. The programme is interesting as affording an idea of the things this unusual vehicle could do as it balanced on its single rail.

The car arrived from its siding, stopped at a platform, and then travelled round the circular track at 20 m.p.h. This accomplished, the car stopped so that the driver could show how it could be tilted to one side or the other for unloading in the field or where lifting tackle was not available. Chocks were provided for the car to lean against. Then parties of fifty were taken round the track, after which the car showed how it could run round curves of as little as 35-ft. radius.

Brennan's monorail car was built as a military vehicle in the first place. He believed that the speed at which the single rail could be laid, combined with the sharp curves which the car could traverse, would make it ideal for military transport. These sharp curves could be vertical as well as horizontal, so that rough country could be crossed. Though the cars could be worked by steam, petrol, or electricity, the idea of military use persuaded Brennan to run his trial car by petrol. This obviated the plume of steam which would give away the car's position in the field.

Two petrol engines, directly coupled to generators, were incorporated. The smaller was of 20 h.p. It supplied current for turning the gyroscopes, operating an air compressor, lighting the train, and travel at low speeds during shunting or when running light. The larger 80 h.p. set was intended to meet power demands beyond the capacity of the smaller set.

Brennan's car was carried on two bogies, each with two wheels. A 40 h.p. motor on each bogie drove one wheel by means of coupling rods, but provision was made for coupling the other wheels if desired. Alternatively, the power could have been increased by providing motors to drive each of the uncoupled wheels, but this would have meant increasing the size of the generators.

Stability was maintained by two gyroscopic wheels rotating in opposite directions at 3,000 r.p.m. The wheels were enclosed in air-exhausted casings and were arranged with their axes of precession vertical and the axes of rotation in the horizontal plane. An unusual lubricating system was installed to feed the shafts of the wheels, which, at the outer ends, were carried in white metal bearings. These were so made that the rotation of the shafts forced a stream of oil, which could be seen like a miniature fountain under a glass dome, along the length of the bearing. It then continued through cooling coils back to a reservoir which held sufficient oil for several months' operation.

This question of free-running of the gyroscopes and their consequent need for constant lubrication was one of the most important factors with which Brennan had to contend. He determined to do away with the need for footstep bearings and this was the main reason why he had horizontal axes for the gyroscopes. He considered, but decided against, the use of roller or ball bearings as requiring too much experimentation to give quick results. Trunnions at the top and bottom of the gyroscope casings allowed them to swing freely about vertical axes on each side of the central position.

A force tending to press the vehicle down on one side caused the cases to precess about their vertical axes, the speed of movement depending on the strength of the sideways movement. Such a force would have been the centrifugal effect on curves. In the Brennan car, the forces used to control precession were derived from compressed air pistons applied to the gyroscope casings. The air was supplied by an electrically-driven compressor. The flow of air was controlled by a completely automatic, but simple mechanism. The gyroscopes controlled the sway of the car, but Brennan for a long time would not reveal the method by which the gyroscopes themselves returned to a central position.

The inertia stored in the gyros was sufficient to keep them revolving for some time after current was turned off, so that there was no danger of any sudden catastrophe. The vehicle would, after a time, lean over very slowly, but there would be ample time to provide props.

Brennan used a single flat-bottom rail, weighing 70 lb. per yd., which was spiked to unballasted fir sleepers. It was slightly more convex than the usual rails used on two-rail lines, but had the advantage of being capable of being laid on longitudinal sleepers. For tramway use, it could be laid flush with the road surface.

Particulars of the trial vehicle, which was, as stated, designed for military purposes and not for comfort or high speeds, were as follows:

Length	40 ft.	Gyro wheel dia.	3 ft. 6 in.
Width	10 ft.	Gyro wheel weight	15 cwt. (each)
Height	13 ft.		
Weight (empty)	22 tons	Brakes	Manual,
Load	10 tons		pneumatic
Rigid wheelbase	5 ft. 4 in.		and electric
Bogie centres	20 ft.	Speed on level	22 m.p.h.

Maximum gradient climbable 1 in 13

Brennan's invention excited great interest and in 1910 he was awarded a Grand Prize by the Japan-British Exhibition at which his car was shown. In 1908 he announced that negotiations were in progress for the adoption of his invention in Australia, and that he hoped to receive assistance from the Australian Government towards his further experiments, but little seems to have come of this.

(*Photo: Régie Autonome des Transports Parisiens*)

(*Above*)   Motor bogie of Paris Métro rubber-tyre train.

(*Below*)   Steam-hauled train of the French National Railways composed of
rubber-tyred lightweight coaches.

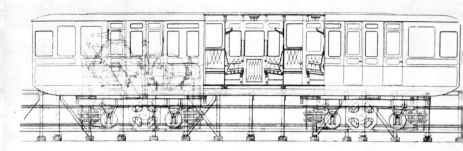

(*Above*) Car designed by Behr for his proposed Liverpool-Manchester high-speed electric railway.

(*Photo: courtesy of Hitchins, Jervis & Partners*)

(*Above*) Model of proposed monorail from Central London to London Airport.

(*Below*) Palmer's railway at Cheshunt on the opening day, with the special passenger car at the front of the train.

Meanwhile, similar work had been going on in Germany, and in 1910 an agreement was drawn up between Brennan and August Scherl of Berlin, the German pioneer, who had taken out his first patent in September 1908, giving Scherl the right to use Brennan patents in Germany and a licence to exhibit his car in the U.S.A. for a limited period. The licence granted to Scherl did not include the latest Brennan patents. Licences were also granted by Brennan to the War Office, the Indian Government, and the Kashmir Government. In return, he received certain subsidies and royalties.

The Scherl gyroscopic monorail car, the demonstration of which in Berlin had brought about Brennan's hasty demonstration, was shown in exhibitions and on trial runs in Brooklyn, New York. The exhibition car had a seating capacity of six, including the motorman, and was thus much smaller than Brennan's machine. It was 18 ft. long and 4 ft. wide and weighed 5,500 lb. Some $5\frac{1}{2}$ per cent of this weight was that of the gyroscopes, which were mounted beneath the car. Like the Brennan gyroscopes, they were enclosed in cases from which the air had been exhausted, but they revolved at a much higher speed than Brennan's—8,000 r.p.m.— and weighed 110 lb. each. They turned in opposite directions and were driven by small electric motors of some $\frac{1}{2}$ h.p. each. The motors were built to run on 115 V.d.c. and were shunt wound. It is stated that the car remained stable even when a passenger was seated on the side and the car circled the Brooklyn track at about 4 m.p.h. The driving power was derived from two 2 h.p. d.c. series motors geared to the wheels of the two two-wheel bogies. The wheels had double flanges and were shaped to conform to the surface of the light 20 lb. track used.

The car leaned over on the curves—rather abruptly, for there was no provision for making it lean before the start of the curve. Current was picked up by two trailing collectors, one on each side of the rear wheel. These made contact with feed wires laid on each side of the rail a few inches away from it and a few inches lower than its surface. Four emergency devices were fitted consisting of rods with rollers at the lower ends. These could be wound down by hand wheels to hold the car upright if current failed or when the car was not in use. Like Brennan's car, the Scherl machine would remain upright for some time after current was cut off under the control of the slowing gyroscopes. Inside-hung brakes were used for normal stops. These demonstrations in early 1910 were the first to be given of monorail capabilities in the U.S.A.

Finally, there was a third true monorail system invented, this time by Peter Schilovsky, a Russian nobleman, Governor of Kostrona. Unlike the others, this never reached the stage of a full-scale demonstration car, but a working model was made by Bassett-Lowke Limited to the designs of the inventor. He used a fairly heavy gyroscope running at 1,500 r.p.m.—much slower than the others—and operating in an air-tight case. The gyroscope revolved in an inclined plane and was arranged so that it could oscillate about a transverse axis. A pendulum transferred any sideways tilt of the train to the gyroscope and amplified it. The reaction of the gyroscope to this urge brought the train back to a level position. This interplay of forces was constant while the gyroscope ran. The model was driven by steam and resembled a Great Northern locomotive in outline. The gyroscope was in the tender, in the normal water space, and water was carried in side tanks in the locomotive itself. A small high-speed steam engine ran the gyroscope, the influence of which was sufficient to balance locomotive, tender, and a trailing coach. The model locomotive weighed 62 lb.

and the gyroscope 10 lb. In 1921-22 the Soviet Government decided on a Schilovsky line from Petrograd to Tsarskoe Seloe, a distance of some 20 miles, but difficulties of finance and the lack of mechanical resources brought work to a halt in 1923.

There was one other form of true monorail, but it was not self-balancing. This was the Caillet monorail. There was only one rail, on which the vehicles ran, but they were supported by men or horses, mules, or donkeys both balancing them and supplying the motive power. These trucks were used in agricultural districts and particularly on plantations. The track—as long as light vehicles were used—was comparatively cheap and gave a much better rolling surface than a plantation road.

An adaptation of this was suggested for use in India, the idea being to lay the rail at the side of the road or in the cess. The vehicle running on it would have had a long beam stretching out to the metalled part of the road and a yoke of oxen would be harnessed to it.

Another adaptation, featured in the *Royal Engineers'* *Journal* in 1917, used a raised rail spiked to posts driven into the ground. A car resembling an Irish jaunting car, with central wheels and carriers hanging pannier-like on each side, would carry the loads and, if evenly loaded, be self-balancing.

The immediate application would have been to carry ammunition and supplies up to the front and bring casualties back, with about 400 lb. in each car. Men walking on duckboards or trench gratings would supply the motive power. The standard Decauville track would have been replaced by this type of line. There is no record of it having been used in actual warfare.

A somewhat more elaborate version of this had been in use for many years in Tunisia and Algeria. This was the invention of C.F.M.T. Lartigue, a Frenchman who had worked on esparto plantations. He mounted his

single rail on a triangular trestle framework, flexible
and light enough to be moved about as required
and curved in any direction. On either side of the
trestles were guiding rails to keep the pannier-like
trucks upright. Some 60 miles of these lines were built
in Algeria and a similar length in Tunisia. They were
operated by mules or horses. The first in Europe
appeared at the Rouen Agricultural Exhibition in
1883.

It may be that Lartigue had seen the invention of J. L.
Hadden, Director of Public Works in Syria, who, in
1869, had invented a monorail to replace mule transport. The rail was placed on a longitudinal beam supported on short posts which could be varied in length
to take up irregularities in the ground or even replaced
by lattice girders when the height became too great for
posts. The wagons and coaches hung in pannier-fashion
from large central wheels. Stability was ensured by
horizontal rollers running on guide rails on the sides of
the posts. The locomotive had a double vertical boiler.
The cost of the line worked out at about £750 a mile and
the train was capable of 25 m.p.h.

In 1894, a Lartigue line, electrically operated, was
opened from Feurs to Panissière in Central France. In
time, Lartigue lines were in use at the Ria mines in the
Pyrenees, near St. Petersburg in Russia, and in Peru and
Guatemala. In 1894, too, a network of electrically-
worked Lartigue lines was planned on Long Island in
the U.S.A., radiating from Brooklyn. For most of their
length the lines would have been at ground level, but in
Brooklyn itself they were to be raised on a series of
"gallows" erected in the centre of suitable streets. London saw a demonstration Lartigue line in 1886, when a
model was built for exhibition near Victoria Street
on part of the site now occupied by Westminster
Cathedral. The portable line shown there could be

easily bent laterally and points were arranged by having a piece of track free at one end which could be moved enough to bring it opposite one track or another as required. It could be fixed by raising it slightly and dropping it into a slot. Where a road had to be crossed, a length of track could be lifted out bodily and replaced as required. Rivers could be crossed by lengthening the legs of the trestles or building light piers, or even supporting the trestles on cables. The track could be bent to give curves of as little as 10-ft. radius and could thus zig-zag up or down slopes as easily as a mountain road.

The light track—part of that built in Tunisia—was suitable for light loads for agricultural or military purposes, but the exhibition also included a much more ambitious steam-worked line. The idea of building this was conceived in April 1886 by Lartigue and he discussed the project with Mallet, the brilliant French locomotive engineer. Plans for the locomotives and carriages, and the heavier rails with their points and crossings, were drawn up. The Westminster ground was obtained on 12 May, and the whole of the equipment was built and ready on 12 July 1886. This time of two months from idea to completion—of an almost totally new system—would be remarkable today and was even more so then.

There were two permanent lines. One was level and intended for experiments as to speed and fuel and water consumption. The other was irregular with steep gradients as severe as 1 in 10, and curves of 49-ft. radius. A turntable gave access from the line to the carriage shed, and here were curves of 32-ft. radius. Every feature that would show the versatility of the system was included, with trestles of varying heights to show how rivers could be crossed and a combination of a 1 in 66 gradient with a curve of 54-ft. radius. There was even a rack section to show how it could be used for mountain lines.

A wooden viaduct 340 ft. in length, with the uprights of the viaduct serving as trestles, was included and a 33-ft. bridge carried one line over the other on the skew. Shunting was performed with switches of flexible track like those of the lighter agricultural line, but because of the greater weight of the track a movable section, 23 ft. in length, was fitted with runners on the sleepers of each trestle to enable it to be moved. A bolt dropping into slots held the track in any of three positions. The bolts could be raised by a lever at the end of the switch lever proper. There were locking fishplates at the free end of the rail and the ends of the fixed lines which it met were fitted with tongues that fitted between the fishplates. A level crossing made use of a similar section free at one end.

The Mallet steam locomotive had two vertical boilers, one hanging on each side of the centre-rail. They were connected by a large pipe which carried the two boilers on the framework and also acted as a steam dome. At the other end was a smaller pipe which allowed water to flow from one boiler to the other and thus maintained a constant level. This pipe was placed low enough to ensure that it always held water and it was only necessary, because of its presence, to feed water to one boiler.

The locomotive had two grooved wheels. Its driver sat astride on a saddle-seat and fed hoppers behind the boilers from buckets of coke carried under his seat. To prevent too great a sway on corners, horizontal guide wheels pressed on longitudinal guides on each side of the trestles. The locomotive weighed $2\frac{1}{2}$ tons and had 15-in. wheels. The cylinders had a 7-in. stroke and were 5 in. in diameter. Boiler pressure was 100 lb p.s.i. and there were 70 super. ft. of heating surface. The tractive capacity was dependent on the gradient, but 70

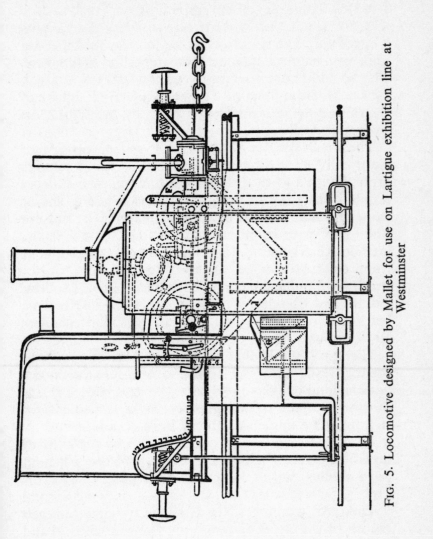

FIG. 5. Locomotive designed by Mallet for use on Lartigue exhibition line at Westminster

tons could be hauled on the level, falling to 18 tons on 1 in 100, 9 tons on 1 in 50, and 6 tons on 1 in 33. Speed was 5–6 m.p.h. but 10–15 m.p.h. could be reached with a light load. The trackwork of the Westminster line was built by Achille Legrand, Mons, and the locomotive, with an additional machine to adapt it for rack working, by La Metallurgique at Tubize in Belgium. The carriages were built at St. Denis, Paris, by the Société des Forges et Ateliers.

The line at the Ria Mines in the Pyrenees was worked electrically. The first trial line was built on broken ground with a 45-deg. slope. The line was four-fifths of a mile in length. At first, the line itself had a 30-deg. slope and was worked by cable haulage. The full line was 6¾ miles in length and was worked by an electric locomotive weighing 1,280 lb. Current was supplied from conductor wires fastened to the sides of the trestles. Four cars could be hauled, each weighing 298 lb. and carrying 990 lb. of ore. The line had no bed plates or sleepers and was carried round curves of 10-ft. radius.

The story is told that Lartigue got his original idea for the trestle monorail from a caravan of camels seen approaching one day in Algeria. He had been thinking of ways in which esparto grass could be carried and the sight of these ungainly animals brought a vision to his mind of the long legs of the camels being replaced by thin trestles, their humps by wheels, and the *thellis*, or huge wallets, which hung down on each side of the camels, by a pannier car.

The great triumph of the Lartigue system was at the mouth of the River Shannon on the west coast of Ireland, in Co. Kerry, where the Lartigue Railway Construction Co. Ltd. built a 9½-mile line from Listowel, a market town on the then Kerry Railway, to Ballybunion on the coast. The line was laid in nine months and opened on 1 March 1888. It was to hold its place throughout its life as the only public passenger-carrying monorail railway in the British Isles.

The main reason for the choice of the Lartigue system for the Listowel & Ballybunion was cheapness, the line costing only £3,000 a mile, including the cost of land, the rolling stock, and the equipment. The whole of the capital was put up by the Lartigue company.

The permanent way consisted of A-shaped trestles some 3 ft. high supported on sleepers buried in trenches cut for them. This system of sunken sleepers obviated any need for ballasting. The vehicles ran on a 27-lb. per yd. steel rail, double headed, and were supported laterally by guide rails on each side of the trestles about 2 ft. 4in. below the main carrying rail, which was in 31-ft. lengths. The trestles were 1 metre apart except at rail joints, where the distance was $\frac{1}{2}$ metre. The angle irons of the supports were bent vertically here to fit under the head and against the web of the rail. The angle irons were bolted together at the joints and the web of the rail made the upper connection. The trestles were not, in general, connected by anything but the rails, but creeping was prevented by a St. Andrew's Cross in each rail length. In places some ballast was needed and longitudinal sleepers were resorted to in boggy places.

The locomotive stock comprised three engines built in 1887 by the Hunslet Engine Company, Leeds. Each engine had two boilers, parallel to each other, and connected with pipes to equalise the water level and steam pressure. Boiler pressure was 150 lb. to the sq. in. The boilers had brass tubes and copper fireboxes, the tube heating surface being 57 sq. ft. and the firebox area $14\frac{3}{4}$ sq. ft. The area of each firegrate was $2\frac{1}{2}$ sq. ft. The two cylinders were of 7-in. dia. and 12-in. stroke. The locomotives were carried on three coupled wheels 2 ft. in diameter, situated between the boilers, the centre wheel being driven.

The tender had two wheels of 2-ft. dia., and a wheel-base of 4 ft. 3 in. The wheels were coupled together, and also to a central driving shaft which could be put into or out of action by a friction clutch. The tender had two cylinders 5 in. in diameter with a stroke of 7 in. The tenders carried 200 gal. of water and 10 cwt. of coal. Engines and tenders were both fitted with the Westinghouse brake, which could be applied from either side. There were also duplicated regulator handles. The total weight of an engine and tender in full working order was 10 tons, the weight of the engine alone being 6 tons. They were painted dark green and could be, and sometimes were, worked up to 27 m.p.h., but the service speed was 18 m.p.h. The Westminster locomotive also was used for a time.

The rolling stock was carried on a single row of wheels, the carriages being built with the lower part in two sections, between which the wheels were placed.

As was to be expected, level crossings caused some difficulty. The principal crossings were made by raising the road to track level and providing drawbridges which preserved the continuity of the road and could be raised to let the trains pass. These crossings were manned, locked, and connected for safety with the signals. Some occupation crossings were of this type, the farmer being given a key to unlock them. As he lowered the roadway by means of chains a signal was automatically put at danger.

Points were formed by mounting a section of line, 25 ft. 6 in. long, on a turntable. The section was bent to a 98·4 ft. radius curve. Trains had to be split and moved a few vehicles at a time over the points, so that operation was slow. There were three parallel lines at Listowel and

Ballybunion, one being used for goods, and two at the intermediate station at Lisselton.

There were 38 vehicles in use, including one first class and seven third class coaches, four composite coaches, and two brake vans, all painted brown. Goods vehicles comprised four goods wagons and 20 sand wagons. The sand wagons were built by Achille Legrand, in Belgium, and the other vehicles at the Falcon works at Loughborough.

Even though the line was in an agricultural district it carried heavy passenger traffic in the summer—as many as 1,400 passengers a day. These were mostly visitors to the district. There was a considerable traffic in sand from some dunes at Ballybunion where the sand happened to be useful as a land dressing and for making mortar. Up to 10,000 tons a year is said to have been carried.

The Newcastle and Tralee branch of the Waterford, Limerick & Western Railway had a station at Listowel near that of the L. & B., and the L. & B. trains, up to five a day in summer, connected with trains from Dublin and Killarney. One difficulty caused by the peculiar divided construction of the coaches was that when they were full on one side passengers had to cross the raised truck to get to empty compartments on the opposite side. Regular passengers crawled under or over the rail, but the official method was to cross by steps carried on two special "platform carriages," one of which was always attached to each train.

Evidence as to the commercial success or failure of the line is conflicting. It passed into the hands of the Official Receiver in 1897, but in 1907 it was declared to be earning a dividend, mostly from the carriage of sand which in the winter was dumped along the line as required by farmers. In 1915, Patrick McCarthy, General Manager of the Listowel & Ballybunion Rail-

way, declared that the line had much helped the rise of
the resort of Ballybunion, an insignificant village when
the line was opened. The line, he said, was self-sup-
porting and made a substantial profit. It needed no
subsidy or guarantee. The first world war and the subsequent rise in costs and the spread of road transport
probably dealt the death blow to the L. & B., and on
14 October 1924, it was closed. Later the line, with its
70 tons per mile of iron and steel, was sold as scrap.

It remained a remarkable effort, and so impressed Sir
H. M. Stanley, the explorer, that he declared that, with
its relative immunity from washaways and burial by
sand-drifts, it should be the only system used in Central
Africa.

A visitor to the L. & B. in 1907, who was allowed to
ride on the footplate, said, "The space at the disposal
of a third person is extremely limited; the driver attends
to the stoking of the engine on his side of the centre rail
and the fireman performs a similar duty with the right
hand firebox; the handles operating the various gear are
in duplicate, so that the locomotive can be controlled
from either footplate.

"The engines are six-coupled, and formerly had two
sets of driving wheels, one for the engine and one for the
tender, but sufficient steam was not generated to propel
all the wheels, and the tender wheels are now uncoupled.
[The driver used a shovel the size of an ordinary kitchen
stove shovel for firing.]

"Travelling on the footplate of a monorail locomotive
is different in many respects from experiences on other
locos. The lookout ahead is widely different, it is somewhat startling to see an apparently fragile trestle
arrangement stretching in front of one, in place of the
usual solid track. The effect is heightened when the line
is formed of a series of sharp reverse curves, the rail then
suggests a monster serpent of interminable length. The

outstanding feature of the monorail footplate is, however, the motion, a speed of 30 m.p.h. is attained, but
long before the locomotive is careering at this rate, the
motion reminds one of riding on a horse attached to a
steam roundabout of the undulating type, working at
full speed, only more so—very much more so, in fact."

At the height of its career extensions to Tarbert and
Ballylongford were propsoed, but these came to nothing.
Before leaving the line we must relate a popular, if
apocryphal, story connected with it. A cow had to be
sent along the line, but there was no load to be put in
the other half of the truck. As the cow could not be
divided, how could the load be balanced?

At first there was much scratching of heads, but
finally someone had a brainwave. Another cow was
borrowed from a farm, put in the other half of the
truck, and the train went off. At the other end of the
line it was suddenly realised that the same problem
remained—how to get the borrowed cow back. With a
touch of genius, the stationmaster borrowed two calves
to balance the cow, and back it went. To get the calves
back was simple. One was placed in each half of the
truck and all was well.

Delegates to the International Railway Congress held
in London in the summer of 1895 visited the L. & B.
railway, and were accompanied by F. B. Behr, Managing Director of the Lartigue Railway Construction
Company. Of Behr a great deal more was soon to be
heard.

Fritz Bernhard Behr, during his long association with
the Lartigue system, formed his own ideas for using the
principle for a high-speed railway. The total freedom
from derailment no doubt encouraged him. There
was only one accident on the Listowel & Ballybunion,
and that was caused by the malicious removal of fasten-
ings for some 30 yards and a sleeper being placed on the

line. Even then, though the obstacle was met by a double-headed train carrying over 200 passengers, all that happened was that the derailed locomotives and coaches "dropped gently to the ground without injury or damage".

Behr saw that a stronger rail would be needed for high speeds and he arranged a stronger trestle carrying a heavy steel rail. This was patented in 1900, the patent description being: "Relates to a support for the rail of a single line railway. The rail is carried on trestle frames having inclined sides of angle iron or steel secured together at the top by a plate riveted to them. The rail is held by a key in a chair, which rests on the top of the trestle and has a downwardly projecting flange which is riveted to the front faces of the trestle bars, and has also two other flanges which are inclined and project down between the trestle bars to the inner webs of which they are riveted."

Behr had had sound training in normal railway practice before he became connected with monorails. He was a pupil of Sir John Fowler during the construction of the original section of the Metropolitan Railway and also worked on the construction of the Midland Great Western Railway of Ireland. His experiments in high-speed traction bore fruit when in 1897, with the encouragement of King Leopold II, Behr built an experimental monorail line, electrically worked, at Terveuren as an annexe to the Brussels Exhibition of 1897.

The line was three miles in length and elliptical in shape. It was a difficult site with bad soil, and heavy engineering works were unavoidable. The line also crossed no fewer than ten roads. The engineering difficulties were not the only ones. Behr was involved in nearly 200 lawsuits with small landowners before he could get the ground at all.

The electric car was enormous, sitting on two four-wheel bogies with skirting hiding the motors and guide wheels at the sides. (Behr's track had five rails. The main monorail was at the apex of the trestles and there were two guide rails on each side of the trestles on which ran the guide rails which prevented sway.) Two wheels in each bogie of the car were driven individually by chains from Parkinson motors of 150 h.p. each. The car thus had a total of 600 h.p. The weight was 55 tons and luxurious seats were provided in long galleries running down either side of the car. On each side were two rows of seats facing each other. This remarkable car was built by the Gloucester Railway Carriage & Wagon Co. Ltd.

All was ready on 14 July 1897, and the Exhibition authorities sent representatives to decide whether Behr's invention merited an award. Unhappily, Behr's troubles were not yet over. As the committee waited, the car straddled its rail quietly—and quietly it stayed there. The power station, a few miles off, newly-built, was unable to supply current.

Once power was available, the high-speed car lived up to its name, careering round the small track at up to 83 m.p.h. Some reports put the speed at up to 100 m.p.h. but the lower figure seems more reliable. Commissioners appointed by the Belgian, Russian, and French Governments to test the car in every possible way, reported that, given a line of sufficient length and a proper power supply, speeds of up to 110–120 m.p.h. could be achieved with safety and moderate expense. This report was a triumph for Behr. His streamlined car, with its special louvres to act as air brakes, had demonstrated that his ideas were based on sound principles.

Behr next became prominent in England. Between Liverpool and Manchester the London & North Western Railway had a monopoly until 1875. In that year the

Cheshire Lines Railway was authorised and when built it joined in the lucrative traffic with a train every hour, covering the 35 miles in 45 minutes. In 1887 the Lancashire & Yorkshire Railway opened its direct route, and in 1900 there was a half-hourly service, counting the three routes, and some 4,500 passengers were carried daily.

A Bill to authorise a high-speed monorail on the Behr system came before Parliament in 1900 and was examined by a select committee headed by Sir John Kennaway. Mr. Balfour Browne, Counsel for the promoters of the Bill, declared that a new line was needed between the two cities every 12 years if the growth of traffic were to be catered for. The mere opposition of existing railways, he declared roundly, could not be allowed to stand in the way of the public being given the service it needed. The existing railways had difficulty in coping with fast and slow traffic on the same lines and would actually benefit by the building of a monorail—possibly alongside existing tracks, for fast traffic could then be separated from slow.

Behr himself gave evidence, speaking "with a strong foreign accent and irresistible loquacity". He spoke of his beliefs and hopes as to "the new phase of traffic" which his monorail system was about to inaugurate. The route, he said, would be from a Manchester terminus at Deansgate, running for more than half the distance parallel to the Cheshire Lines Railway. There would be a different entrance to Manchester because he thought that of the Cheshire Lines Railway to be "a bad one" and because of the "trifling obstacle" offered by the Manchester Ship Canal. A generating station would be built for the line at Warrington, about halfway along the route. The Liverpool terminus was to be at Church Street, in the centre of the town. To queries about the effect of his elevated structures on the appear-

(Photo: Wuppertaler Schwebebahn.

(*Above*).   Train crossing new span across new highway and River Wupper,
Wuppertal Schwebebahn (Suspended Railway).

(*Below*).   Train leaving intermediate station of the Wuppertal Schwebebahn.

(Photo: Carl Bellingrodt.

(*Above*)   The Bennie Railplane at a station.

(*Below*)   Bennie track over an orthodox railway near Glasgow.

ance of the towns he replied that he had "selected the very worst property in Salford for his line to pass through" but 45 streets would have to be crossed.

Support came from the Lord Mayor of Manchester, who spoke of the advantage to cotton spinners of trains every 10 minutes taking only 20 minutes over the journey. A well-known engineer, Mr. R. Elliott Cooper, gave evidence that he had no doubt of the feasibility of Behr's proposals.

Nevertheless, the committee rejected the Bill. In doing so, however, it expressed the opinion that "the monorail system, when fully matured, is likely to make an important contribution to the development of railway traffic at high speed", but, it said, no safe method of applying brake power to these very high speed trains had yet been demonstrated. This alone was enough to make practical men conclude that "electrical express railway carriages are at present in an experimental stage."

The promoters of the line had no such doubts. In an interview with a representative of the *Liverpool Journal of Commerce* in 1900, one of them said: "The block system of the Electric Express will be infinitely superior to anything now in existence. Signals, for one thing, will be done away with—at least, the signals which now wave their arms mysteriously and are invisible in a fog. The Electrical Expresses cannot 'telescope' each other in the rear, or crash into each other like mad bulls head to head, while splintered carriages are piled sky-high, and the blood and the groans of the dead and the dying issue from the mangled mass of wood and iron. The conductor of the Electrical Express has a dial before him, the sensitive pointers on which tell him exactly how far the train before him is in front, and how far the train behind him is in the rear, fog or no fog; the apparatus locates an obstruction on the line as accurately

as the Post Office officials find out a break in the telegraph wires; consequently the Electric Express is safety
itself. As for curves, they present no difficulty. The
express can wriggle round them with the greatest ease."

A less "wriggly" defence came from Sir W. H. Preece
in one of the most important papers in the Mechanical
Science Section of the British Association meeting in
Bradford in September 1900. He implied that a new
scheme would be put before Parliament which would
avoid, the "inconveniences" of the earlier plan. The
train he announced, would consist of one coach only,
weighing 45 tons, and seating 64. Trains would start
every 10 minutes and travel at a mean rate of 110 m.p.h.
The $34\frac{1}{2}$ miles would be covered in 20 minutes. The
fares would be slightly lower than those charged by the
railways. There would be no intermediate stations and
no points or crossings. The Warrington power station
would supply current at 15,000 V. This would be
carried to both terminals and there stepped down to
the working voltage of 650 V.

Behr himself followed with a paper on the brakes and
signals to be adopted. No train, he said, would leave
Manchester or Liverpool until the train in front had
reached Warrington—17 miles away.

The line would be divided for signalling into eight
sections of 4·3 miles each. As the train left Manchester,
a danger signal was put up automatically at that station.
A second signal went to danger at 4·3 miles, the first
remaining at danger. A third signal went to danger at
8·6 miles. Simultaneously, the signal at Manchester
(or Liverpool as the case might be) was lowered. A
second train could then leave when required.

Assuming that the first train met with trouble after
the 8·6-miles signal, the second train would travel at
normal speed to the 4·3-mile signal. This would be at
danger and the driver would know he had to stop, but

he would have 4·3 miles in which to bring the train to a stand. This could be done, if necessary, simply by cutting off the current and without using the brakes. A six-minute service could be run, he declared, and by halving the block lengths a three-minute service could be run, the trains still having at least 2·15 miles in which to stop.

The rejection of the scheme did not stop Behr's supporters. Parliament was asked to pronounce on an amended scheme for a railway of 34 miles, 3 furlongs, 3 chains in length from the west side of Deansgate, Manchester, to School Lane, Liverpool (near the Bluecoat Hospital). This line was a furlong shorter than that of the previous scheme and the cost was estimated at £1,776,821 compared with the original £1,748,940.

After a lengthy enquiry, the House of Lords Committee, headed by Viscount Falkland, decided that the Bill could go forward provided that the promoters would guarantee that the centre of gravity of the cars would be at least 12 in. below the top of the running rail. Dr. E. Hopkinson, an expert witness, said he had no doubt whatever as to the possibility of running the cars at the proposed speed of 110 m.p.h. He calculated that a speed of 110 m.p.h. could be attained in just over two minutes from starting, the distance covered in the meantime being just under two miles. During the time of acceleration he estimated that the maximum electrical power required would be about 1500 h.p. It was quite possible to transmit that power from a central generating station. A rapid rate of retardation, as well as a rapid rate of acceleration, would be necessary. If 3 ft. per second were applied as the rate of retardation, the train would be brought to rest from a speed of 110 m.p.h. in considerably under one mile of distance and in 54 seconds. He thought this rate would be a proper rate to choose in ordinary working on approaching the terminus. It would be possible to apply a much greater rate of retardation if necessary. There were many instances on record of trains being suddenly pulled up at the rate of 8 or 9 ft. per second. It would be very undesirable to pull up at that rate, but it was possible.

It was suggested that the passengers might be projected out through the windows by centrifugal force, but this particular objection seems to have been overcome!

The Bill then went to the Commons, where a Select Committee, presided over by Sir Lewis McIver, decided by a majority to pass it on condition that the promoters accepted conditions similar to those of light railways and tramways, binding them, before construction, to submit for the approval of the Board of Trade plans and other details of construction and material in respect of permanent way, rolling stock, mode of working, electrical installations, system of signalling and of braking, and so on.

The hearings of the committees took 39 days in all and 84 witnesses were examined, but on 17 August 1901, the scheme was authorised as the Manchester & Liverpool Electric Express Railway.

The Behr railway needed five rails, one being the main track and the remainder guide rails, two on each side resting longitudinally on the trestles. The trestles were to lie on ordinary wood railway sleepers 9 ft. long, 10 in. wide, and 5 in. deep, lying cross-wise. The trestles were 3 ft. 11½ in. high and 2 ft. 8 in. wide at the base, narrowing to 12 in. at the tip. The main steel monorail was single-faced in 35-ft. lengths and weighed 103½ lb. to the yard. The guide rails weighed 30½ lb. and were double-headed.

Access to the Deansgate and School Lane termini would have been by lift. Three classes of carriage were envisaged, holding 72, 50, and 38 passengers. The overall length would have been 41 ft. 10 in., the width 11 ft., and the internal height from floor to roof 6 ft. $8\frac{1}{4}$ in. Pointed ends were designed to reduce wind resistance. The carriages had a main steel central frame which formed the lower part of the vehicle. It fitted over the rail and came down to within 6 in. of the soleplate of the trestles on each side.

Four continuous current motors of 160 h.p. at a working speed of 720 r.p.m. drove the car, and were able to work up to an output of 320 h.p. for short periods, giving rapid acceleration. The motors were arranged in pairs at either end of the carriage, one on each side, and weighed $2\frac{1}{4}$ tons each. Their low position gave stability to the 39-ton cars, and this stability was reinforced by the four guide wheels on each side. These, by running with the flanges below the edges of the guide rails, locked the carriages to the track and made derailment, for all practical purposes, impossible.

This sounds as though the carriages were rigidly fixed, with all the rough riding that would go with it, but, in fact, springs were fitted to give vertical and lateral play. The four track wheels were made up of two 4 ft. 4 in. driving wheels, with chain drive from the motors, and two trailing wheels 3 ft. 5 in. in diameter.

A feature of the track of interest was the proposed steep gradient at both ends of the line: 1,200 yd. of 1 in 30 at the Manchester end and 1 in 25 at Liverpool. The idea was to give rapid acceleration for trains leaving the stations and similarly rapid deceleration entering.

In January 1902 an estimate was lodged in Parliament referring to a deviation of the route through Salford, where, it will be recalled, many streets had to be crossed. This included £111,000 for a covered way. Before this could be dealt with, Behr discovered that the Salford Corporation had built, or had allowed to be built, a number of houses on the proposed route.

eventually agreement was reached and the Corporation withdrew its objections to the deviation.

The Board of Trade, however, had considerable doubts about the braking system for Behr's very high-speed vehicles. It would be thought that with Behr's evidence that the trains could stop without brakes if necessary, and the fitting of two Westinghouse brakes able to stop the car in 800 yd. from 110 m.p.h., the Board would have been satisfied. Behr's addition of his louvred air brakes and an electric brake consisting of small dynamos connected with the driving wheels would have appeared to put the matter beyond doubt. The combined brakes could, in theory, stop the car in 500 yd. from 110 m.p.h.

The Board of Trade was still doubtful, and in December 1902 the promoters of the railway offered, not for the first time, to build seven miles of the railway near Warrington to let the Board see the monorail at work before giving sanction for the whole line.

In May 1903 the "Mono Rail Construction Company, Limited" was registered at Somerset House to issue the capital for the line. The capital of the company was £60,000, all privately subscribed. In fact, however, the full capital for the construction was never raised, and the scheme petered out gradually. By 1906 the project had been abandoned.

While the attempt to find capital went on Behr had not been idle. A scheme for a London–Brighton electric line of normal pattern failed on Standing Orders in Parliament in 1902, and a scheme for a Behr monorail was being canvassed. Behr had prepared a pamphlet as far back as 1893 to show that his monorail could be built beside the normal line to Brighton at a cost of less than £1,000,000, for a double track. Speeds of 150 m.p.h. were possible, he said, and Brighton could be reached in 20 minutes. If continued on the other side of the Channel, he maintained, his line would bring Paris within three hours of London. This presumably did not count the time needed for the sea crossing.

In a leading article in *Transport* for 10 January 1902, it was said of a pamphlet "London to Brighton by Steam and Electricity", issued by the promoters of the London and Brighton Electric Railway, that "At first glance the representation of the train looks more like one of the war machines as familiarised in Mr. H. G. Wells' widely read 'War of the Worlds'. . . One thing at least will be of interest, viz., the arrangements which are proposed for the trains 'leaving the station to cross Grosvenor Road on a girder'. I am very exercised in my mind as to how the promoters have estimated their loads—and their revenue—as they say on page 18 that 'each carriage when loaded will weigh about 50 tons. That the first-class carriages will accommodate between 30 and 50 passengers, and the third-class about 100 passengers.' But as it is stated on page 14 that 'the customers of the railway are sure to be enormous' I should rather be inclined to think that they have founded their estimate of revenue as regards passengers more on weight than at per head."

In April 1902 a syndicate commissioned Behr to plan a London–Brighton monorail. Early in 1903 it was announced that the line would start from Westminster. Capital powers for £4,500,000 in share capital and £1,500,000 in debentures were to be sought. Passenger fares were not to exceed 2d. a mile first class and 1d. a mile second class. There was to be no third class.

The existing railway, the London Brighton & South Coast, promptly sought powers to electrify its own lines and prepared a memorial of 123 pages protesting that the Bill for the monorail did not comply with Parliamentary Standing Orders. In particular, it mentioned a difficulty in raising the requisite deposit of some £200,000.

The cost of the monorail was estimated at £4,394,927 —about £87,898 per mile. The promoters asked for the option of refusing to carry goods. The proposed directors were Mr. G. C. Montague, M.P., Mr. Thomas Newcomer, Sir Frederick Forestier-Walker, and Mr. Arthur Woolley Hart. The London terminus was named as Clare Street, St. Clement Danes. The last word of this scheme came only a few days later. At the half-year annual meeting of the London Brighton & South Coast Railway it was said that the Behr monorail "was proceeded with until the very day when memorials against it had to be lodged in Parliament, but the engineer and solicitor were able to formulate so formidable a set of allegations of non-compliance with Standing Orders that the promoters did not care to face the enquiry and they have consequently retired from the contest".

Across the Atlantic, Behr made one more bid for recognition. One of the features of the British Section at the St. Louis World's Fair in 1904 was to be a large working model of his system, towards the cost of which the British Commission was reported to have voted £200. A "One-Rail Traction Co. of New York" was incorporated in New Jersey with a capital of $125,000 to "buy and sell patent rights for an auto-balancing system of one-rail railroads".

The model was constructed by the Model Manufacturing Company and embodied all Behr's latest improvements, including horizontal guide wheels arranged to move in radial slotted bearings instead of being bolted rigidly to the bogies. This allowed a certain lateral movement of the car which could be controlled at will, and obviated the need to incline the track on curves. Current was fed from the rails by wheels pressed to the conductors by springs, instead of the original shoes. The model, which excited much interest, was on a scale of $\frac{3}{4}$ in. to 1 ft. It was Behr's last appearance in the public eye.

The last major system to be discussed is that of Mr. E. W. Chalmers Kearney, publicly introduced in June 1908 after a series of experiments over the preceding six years. The Kearney trains ran on one rail, as did Brennan's, but the balancing function was performed by a second rail running over the train. The inventor proposed that this overhead rail should be braced and supported by standards at 60-ft. intervals. The centre of gravity of the cars was to be kept low, and the pressure on the overhead guide wheels could consequently be small even when the car was standing and almost disappear when speed was gained. An automatic adjustment ensured that the guide wheels could not leave the top rail and a telescopic arrangement in the columns connecting the running and guide rail bogies compensated for variation in vertical gauge.

The saving in cost on orthodox construction may be seen from the estimate of £99,000 for a Kearney line from Herne Hill to the Crystal Palace against £207,900 for an ordinary railway. In operation, the use of ball-bearings on all moving parts of the car ensured the minimum of friction, and the power required for the electric motors (which picked up current from a trolley wire attached to the guide-rail structure) was less than 20 per cent of that needed for an orthodox coach. Later arrangements were made for the current to be taken from the upper rail.

It was claimed that the system was particularly suitable for tube railways because of its ability to surmount steep gradients, and it was in this direction that it showed the greatest promise. Kearney proposed to site his platforms immediately below the street. The line would be in a 14-ft. dia. tube which would fall abruptly at 1 in 7 from the stations. This would allow rapid acceleration and deceleration. It was estimated that in 210 yd. and 19 seconds from a station, the train would be 90 ft. down. In 20 seconds from starting it would be travelling at working depth at some 50 m.p.h.

Objections that passengers would feel nervous at such steep gradients, using only adhesion, were met by the contention that the forces of acceleration and deceleration would counterbalance the effect of the gradients.

Assuming stations on such a line to be 1,100 yd. apart, the train would run from the downward gradient on to a level stretch of 600 yd., which would be covered in 24 seconds, and then up a similar 1 in 7 gradient. A stop of no more than 15 seconds was assumed and it was thought that if there were platforms on each side of the car, the passengers passing out at one side and entering at the other, even this time could be cut considerably.

Lines were proposed from Cricklewood to the Oval *via* Marble Arch and Victoria, and from the Strand to Crystal Palace *via* Waterloo, the Oval, and Herne Hill. Kearney said that if existing tubes had been built on his system, even the poorest of them would be paying 10 per cent on the ordinary stock. One factor was the reduced cost of his system, which avoided the need for lifts and shafts at the sub-surface stations, and another the saving in power needed for acceleration, which would be taken care of by the gradients. The gradients would also have avoided the need for excessive braking. The high speed of the Kearney line would have enabled each car to do more work, and fewer cars, and consequently fewer staff, would have been needed to work an intensive service than with a normal tube line.

Kearney had other ideas, too, for his system. A Kearney Elevated was proposed for New York. It was to have light cars carried on a light, graceful track overhead which would leave the view of the sky almost unobstructed. Then there was the Kearney Express Parcels Service which was to use a 2-ft. dia. tube and have driverless trains. At the Crystal Palace a model Kearney line appeared in action with cars 44 in. in length over buffers. These were to a scale of ¾in. to the foot and reversed automatically at each end of the track. They also had self-acting track brakes.

In 1902 Kearney proposed an electric express route from the City to a new seaside town on the south coast—actually a "garden city". This would be, he said, only a 30-35 minute run in his trains. Because of its ability to tackle steep gradients, the monorail could cross both the North and South Downs with the minimum of engineering work. Model garden towns 40 miles from London would be only half an hour away in time.

On 7 January 1925, a new chapter opened when Colonel Moore-Brabazon (now Lord Brabazon), who was then Parliamentary Secretary to the Ministry of Transport, received a deputation representing the Middlesex and Essex County Councils, and other councils and public bodies in the London area, which had come to urge the construction of a Kearney tube. Colonel Moore-Brabazon was so interested that he wrote in a letter published in *The Times* the next day that he had been impressed by Kearney's advocacy of his system and recommended an application for a light railway on the Kearney plan. The Trade Facilities Committee, he believed, would probably guarantee the interest on the capital. Lord Headley, President of the Kearney Society, told Moore-Brabazon that there were two suggested schemes, one of which was a half-mile tube between North and South Shields, and the other a ¾ mile North Woolwich–Woolwich line.

The outcome of all this was the promotion of the North and South Shields Tube Railway under the Light

Railways Act. An inquiry was held locally at South Shields in February and March 1926, and in June 1927 the Minister of Transport announced that he would bring in a Bill to confirm the provisional order.

The line had been projected, as an orthodox tube railway, in 1914, with a Mr. John Portsmouth as engineer. Mr. Portsmouth had tried to revive the scheme in 1921, but the cost was prohibitive, and he therefore handed the whole scheme over to Kearney and recommended his system. Kearney drew up plans in 1923 for a single tube under the Tyne to be worked by a shuttle service. The 1 in 7 gradients were incorporated and the line was to have been 42 ft. beneath the bed of the river. The car was expected to make the journey in 50 seconds. The estimated cost was £300,000, but Kearney said that if only 5,000,000 passengers a year were carried at 2d. each he could show a profit of £31,000.

However, in 1928 Tynemouth opposed the enabling Bill at the committee stage and it was rejected, apparently because it was felt that there was not enough financial evidence to judge the scheme but also because it was thought that any tube railway should connect the two London & North Eastern Railway stations. This latter point was met by Kearney in a new plan and the L.N.E.R. agreed to the scheme in 1932. By this time, North and South Shields were clamouring for a road tunnel instead, but the Minister of Transport would not agree.

Kearney tried again, but the two Corporations turned his scheme down even after a London firm, Arthur Whitley Limited, had offered to finance and build his line. A 1939 attempt was made by the North & South Shields Electric Railway Co. to promote the tube as a light railway and to build it without cost to the local authorities. The platforms would have been on the same level as those of the L.N.E.R. The coming of the second world war prevented this scheme from reaching fruition, but at the time of writing (1956) Mr. Kearney was still a patient advocate of his high-speed railway, which undoubtedly has many attractive features, and at one time excited interest overseas, including a proposed line between Venice and Venice Lido. A working model was exhibited at 51, Aldwych, London, in 1908, and at the London Louvre, Oxford Street, in 1912, when it was announced that a Kearney line was to be built between Nice and Monte Carlo. This would have covered the 11 miles in 20 minutes. There would have been seven intermediate stations. The line would have started as a gravity tube opposite the Casino in the Place de Massena and continued in tube for $1\frac{1}{4}$ miles. The line would then have run on the surface for nine miles and descended for a final $\frac{3}{4}$ mile in tube to the Place du Casino, Monte Carlo. Where possible, the contours of the ground would have been followed. The double track would have cost £5,000 a mile less than an ordinary railway.

A full-size Kearney car was built by Brush and illustrated in a railway journal in 1912. It was 45 ft. in length, 8 ft. wide, and had 7 ft. 6 in. headroom in the centre aisle. The ends were tapered, outside sills were eliminated and frameless windows used. All these features contributed to streamlining. The car, which had seats for 45 passengers, had at one end a private compartment with tables, a tea cupboard, and a concealed washbasin. At the other end were lounge seats. The main body of the car had transverse seats. Driving compartments were incorporated beyond the private compartment at one end and the lounge at the other. This car was eventually destroyed by fire.

The two bogies had four 36-in. wheels each, and each wheel was motor-driven.

When the Moscow Underground was projected,

Kearney visited Moscow, and it was announced that the Moscow authorities had accepted the Kearney system for use on the projected lines. This report was unfounded.

Perhaps the last important news was heard of the Kearney system when it was pointed out in 1939 that Kearney tubes could make excellent air raid shelters. The single rail left plenty of room for two tiers of seats running longitudinally along the tube on both sides, and the fact that the single rail could be sunk flush with the floor and the conductor rail was safely in the roof of the tunnel made the tubes safe for pedestrians and those taking shelter when the trains were not running. Some 16,000 persons could shelter in a mile of tube and sit on the tiers of seats. A further 9,000 could stand in the centre. Thus a double-track tube could shelter 50,000 people per route mile.

It was thought that such a railway could be built for £500,000 a mile, giving a figure for shelter purposes of £10 a head compared with the £50 a head being quoted at the time for deep shelters of the normal type. Also, the railway would earn revenue in normal times and thus at least help to pay for itself.

Other monorails of elevated types are discussed in another chapter. The dividing line is often thin, but this chapter is already long. Before leaving it, however, there must be mentioned a monorail built at Kilmarnock by the Rev. R. R. Thom. This line appears to be almost unknown, and we think it worth while quoting in full the report which appeared in the *Kilmarnock Standard* for 4 June 1904.

"THE MARVO RAILWAY

"At the present time an urgent demand is being made for increased speed in locomotion. To meet this in connection with railways very large engines have been built but these have not answered the problems as well as had been expected. It has involved much expense both in construction and upkeep and the combined weight of engines, coals and water, and carriages has been greatly out of proportion to the weight of passengers carried, and the gain in speed not worth the increased expense. In the Marvo system (invented by the Rev. R. Riach Thom) the idea is to employ stationary engines and electric traction with light carriages.

"From the construction of the Marvo Railway such carriages can be used with perfect safety. In this new system of locomotion two rails are employed, an under bearing rail and an upper guiding rail. The inventor having noticed that hoops and bicycles running freely at speed, automatically retain an upright position, concluded that a carriage running on a single rail would observe the same laws, and consequently that the upper wheels would exert very little side strain on the guiding rail.

"It was found by experiment that if the under wheels were double grooved so as to run on a rail with a convex upper surface, and the guide rail formed one continuous groove, in section approaching to the shape of the capital letter U turned upside down, the guide wheel running within it would on a straight track scarcely ever touch the inside of the rail. As friction is thus reduced to a minimum the greatest possible speed becomes attainable.

"Along with the maximum of speed, this system combines a special provision for safety. On ordinary railways the wheels have about an inch of flange and that on the inner side only. In the Marvo the flanges are four times as deep, or more. There are other advantages consequent on this impossibility of derailment. Light cars can be used which will need much less driving power than heavy cars, and having, when in motion, far less momentum, will be much more easily and quickly brought to a standstill.

"In the case of the Marvo line having to cross a road, a river, or ordinary railway track, the lightness of the cars is of great advantage, as a light viaduct will be sufficient to carry the weight. In addition to these advantages the cars run across their own rails at level crossings without the aid of shifting points, and without any unsteadiness or jolt. As the Marvo can take steep gradients and go round extreme curves, there will be less need than in ordinary railways for tunnels, cuttings, and embankments. Instead of sending on large trains at remote intervals, small trains or single carriages can be sent one after another as speedily as required. By means of automatic electric signals, collisions through one train or carriage overtaking another that might come to a stand would be effectually prevented. The system is equally adapted for tramways.

"From its many advantages over other systems, the Marvo promises to be the railway of the future. In speed it will be an inestimable boon to travellers who in a comparatively short space of time would be enabled to reach their homes at any hour of the day.

"To demonstrate the wonderful capabilities of this system, a working model, with carriages and an electric motor, was constructed by Messrs. T. McCall & Sons, 3, High St., Kilmarnock. The course was an endless one in shape like the figure 8. This wrought so well that Mr. H. MacIndoe, the well known and enterprising caterer for the entertainment and recreation of the public, having inspected it gave an order for the construction of a similar railway capable of carrying about 150 passengers. He stipulated, however, that it should possess a little of the switchback element, by being built with varying gradients.

(*above*)
"mock-up" of Skyway Monorail
coach, Houston, Texas.

(*right*)
Skyway Monorail demonstration
line at Houston.

(*Photo: Peter Whitney*)

(*Photo: Kent & Sussex Couri

(*Above*)   Brockhouse "Uniline" train.

(*Below*)   Model of Alweg monorail near Cologne.

(*Photo: Associated Pre*

"The length of the line was to be 220 ft., the length of the figure from end to end 77 ft., the greatest breadth 33 ft. and the gradient to be not less than 1 in 12, rising from the level crossing in the middle towards each end. The carriages had to be of restricted height in order to enable them when placed on railway trucks for transport to pass under bridges. The difficulty in contriving such a line, whereas a passenger railway on the same system would be mere child's play in comparison. All these difficulties, however, have been overcome, and the railway, now completed, and in operation, effectually demonstrates the wonderful capabilities of the system.

"As a matter of course, it is impossible to get up any great speed upon such a line of such extreme curvature and if it were possible, it would not be desirable. The verdict of experts who have examined this railway is that the system has a great future before it. It is confidently anticipated that in the matter of speed it will be superior to all existing systems. The inventor, the builders, and the proprietor are all to be congratulated in the successful completion of the work."

Not dissimilar was an earlier venture in America, Boynton's Bicycle Railway at Brighton Beach, New York. In his system the lower rail rested on the ground and the upper rail was immediately above it, supported at intervals by large hoops. Small horizontal guide wheels above the locomotive and coaches bore against the sides of the upper rail.

The steam locomotive had a single driving wheel, 7 ft. $10\frac{1}{2}$ in. in diameter, driven by two cylinders. The engine and tender formed a single unit, two small wheels supporting the tender portion. The coaches had two decks, one above the other, and ran on bogies, each of which had two wheels in tandem.

CHAPTER NINE

OVERHEAD RAILWAYS

THE idea of overhead railways, supported on stilts of one kind or another, occurred to railway engineers very early. The chief attraction was probably that by varying the length of the legs of the stilts it was possible to cross undulating ground without any of the costly earthworks which would be needed on an orthodox railway line. In later years the idea has had continued attraction in densely populated areas because it offers the possibility of building railways without sterilising the whole of the valuable ground over which they pass.

In this chapter we shall not deal with orthodox railways built on viaducts, though there are many examples, nor shall we deal with cable railways, which, fascinating as they are, are not really railways. Even without these, the chapter will be long and varied, for ideas on the subject have been many.

The first proposal for an overhead suspended railway seems to have come from an Englishman, Henry Robinson Palmer, who was Engineer to the London Dock Company. Not unnaturally, he turned his idea, which he patented in 1821, to the loading and unloading of vessels. His first line was built, probably in 1824, to carry goods between the Thames and the warehouses of the Royal Victualling Yard. The practicability of his system was advocated in a book which he published in 1823 called "Description of a Railway on a New Principle". This must have been popular as it went into a second edition in the following year.

The new principle he expounded was that a single

rail should be supported in the air on stout wooden posts. The height would vary according to the undulations of the ground below. The rail itself was made of planks set on edge and held in notches in the tops of the posts. The running surface was protected by an iron bar, convex on its upper surface, laid on top of the rail. The supporting posts were of oak from ships' timbers and were 7½ in. ×4 in. They were spaced, with some variation, about 10 ft. apart. A second line followed on the same principle in 1825. This carried bricks across the Cheshunt marshes from the brickworks to waiting barges on the River Lee (commonly spelt "Lea").

The vehicles were carried on two cast-iron wheels with deep flanges. The wheels were 26 in. in diameter and the vehicles were divided, like those on the Listowel & Ballybunion Railway, half a century later, so that they hung down on each side and balanced. Each side of the wagons had a capacity of 20 cu. ft. The trains consisted, as far as old prints can be relied on, of seven cars. These were drawn by a horse pulling on a tow rope—probably suggested by the normal horse haulage of barges.

For the grand opening of the Cheshunt Railway on 25 June 1825, a carriage was constructed "in the barouche style" and duly carried the company along the line. After this, the "elegant" carriage vanished into obscurity and it is almost certain that no other passengers were ever carried on the line.

Palmer's railway proved a stimulus to thought, and in 1824 one Luke Herbert suggested in the *Register of the Arts and Sciences* that the railway should be used with sail power as an auxiliary. He also suggested a Palmer railway between London and Brighton for the transport of fish.

In 1826 Palmer exhibited a model of his railway at Elberfeld and a company was formed to carry coal between Elberfeld and Barmen on a Palmer line. No construction was ever undertaken, but it is a curious coincidence that an overhead railway, which will be described later in this chapter and is still working, should be built on this route some three-quarters of a century later.

After the Palmer railway there is a long gap in the story of overhead railways, though it must not be forgotten that other systems mentioned in this book were capable of being used in this fashion, and that our splitting into chapters is to a great extent a matter of personal preference. However in the U.S.A. in 1877 there appeared at the Philadelphia Exhibition a single-rail railway which was the invention of a Mr. Le-Roy Stone.

Stone's rail rested on longitudinal sleepers made of wood, supported at intervals by cast-iron pillars. As in Palmer's system, the frames of locomotives and carriages were brought down pannier-fashion on each side of the track. There was an advance on the Palmer system in that the frames carried two horizontal wheels on each side which bore against channel irons carried on a framework from the longitudinal sleepers. Stone's system thus resembled Lartigue's.

The locomotives had only two vertical wheels, the rear wheel being the driver. Power was provided from a rotary engine supplied with steam from an ordinary boiler. The balancing of the locomotive was ensured by side tanks, hung below the rail level, which carried water and coal. The size of the train may be judged from the fact that the carriages had two passenger levels.

In Wales, in 1880 a Mr. Collett of Cardiff produced plans for an overhead railway which embodied a principle that has since been widely adopted for overhead railways. He suspended his locomotive and coaches from wheels running on a rail above the train and supported by pillars as necessary. He proposed steam traction for his line, but it appears to have progressed no further than the design stage.

The following year, in Germany, Heussinger von Waldegg, a German engineer, proposed the use of tree stumps to support forestry railways. The stumps would have supported cross-members on which would rest wooden longitudinals. These would have had angle irons mounted on them on which the wheels of the forestry trucks would run. In passing, it may be said that in the early days in both the United States and Canada, wooden longitudinals were used as rails, without iron protection; one example was the 100-mile long Lewis & Kennebec Railway. Australia also had lines of this type.

The Railway Engineer in 1885 reported that a M. Angely had produced a plan for a suspended railway in Paris. In the Angely system two overhanging girders were supported by a single row of columns eight metres above the ground. The girders carried two rails, themselves of girder section. The wheels of the carriages were arranged two and two on each side of the rail.

The columns were 32 metres apart and 12·5 metres high, and made of sheet-iron 12 mm. thick. They were fixed by foundation bolts to blocks of solid concrete. The girders were supported at three points between the columns by ties fixed to the tops of the columns. To make them more rigid they were also braced together by transverse and diagonal braces. Traction could be by wire rope, steam, or electricity. The stations would have been in houses at the sides of the streets, with short bridges leading to the trains. Paris, however, appears to have shown no great delight in this ingenious system.

In 1886 a company in Boston, U.S.A., obtained a charter to construct one mile of a one-rail elevated railway in the city of Cambridge, Massachusetts. An engine and carriage adapted to the system were also to be built. The line was a trial one for the benefit of the Railroad Commissioners. If their approval had been obtained, the company was to be allowed to build such overhead railways in Boston with the permission of the city government. A description in *The Railway Engineer* says:

"The structure consists of a single rail elevated on a line of posts 14 ft. from the ground. It is called a single rail, though perhaps a more correct description would be two rails placed one above the other at a distance of four feet and connected by a series of braces. The supports or posts are placed at distances of 45 ft. and are almost exactly like those of the New York Elevated Railroad, except that the lower end is firmly encased in concrete and rests on a solid bed of concrete several feet underground.

"The truck frame of the cars is placed astride the rail, like a saddle on the back of a horse, and each truck frame has six wheels. On either side, two of these wheels run on the lower part of the rail, inclining upward and outward from the point of contact at an angle of 45 deg. The other two wheels are placed horizontally under the car and level with the top of the rail, along the sides of which they run, one on each side. By means of hydraulic pressure applied from the engine, they are made to clasp the rail tightly, and by this power of traction the forward or backward movement is secured. Each wheel has an independent axis of its own, and the opposing wheels are always kept at right angles with the rails, regardless of sharp curves. Steep grades may be overcome by means of the traction power.

"The truck frames of the locomotive are like those of the car, with the connecting rods attached to the horizontal wheels on either side of the rails. The pressure of the wheels on the rail is such as to make it almost impossible for them to leave it, but in case this should happen the car could not leave the track, but would drop 1½ in. and slide along, resting on the top of the rail, the truck frame serving as a substantial brace on both sides. The cars are cylindrical in form, and built of iron."

In 1895 a Bill was put forward by the National Transit Company for a monorail on the Brolt system from New York to Washington. The tracks were to have been elevated and the trains were expected to be capable of 120 m.p.h. The carriages were to be of steel and vulcanised rubber. Gearless electric motors were to have been used, the current being collected by an overhead trolley.

In May 1897 a Mr. Halford produced an invention "relating to elevated railways or railways for recreational purposes". There was to be a single overhead rail, and —again carrying on the pannier idea—two compartments would be suspended from each trolley running on the rail. The trolley controlled, automatically, hydraulic apparatus by which the rails were successively elevated to produce a gradient down which the cars ran by gravity.

We can do no better than to quote the impressions of the Editor of *The Railway Engineer* when he saw the railway at work later in the year. He said:

"We were lately afforded an opportunity of inspecting a working model of this type of railway. In order to introduce the system to the public it is intended to erect recreation lines, but subsequently the inventor hopes that it may be generally used in place of the ordinary railway.

"The lines are raised at any convenient height above the ground, in order that the cars, which are suspended on pivots attached to a bogie, may clear the ground. The line consists of girders resting at both ends on hydraulic rams. When the train is ready to start, one end of the girder on which it rests is raised and the train runs down, and as it approaches the other end of the girder its weight depresses it and automatically turns on the pressure into the hydraulic cylinder, which begins to rise immediately the train has passed.

"In a full-size train the working of the hydraulic cylinders would be controlled from the cars by means of electricity. The inventor claims that a speed of 200 m.p.h. could be safely attained and maintained. The novelty of this invention is startling and its ingenuity remarkable. The model, which was about 7 yards long and had a straight and level line, worked quite satisfactorily.

"Locomotive engineers, however, can hardly be expected to look with favour on the invention, as simultaneously with its adoption the necessity for their department would disappear. We look forward with pleasure to a ride on one of these railways, as tobogganing for a hundred miles or so in a comfortable attitude would be exhilarating."

It is to be regretted that, as the line was never built, the editor did not get his wish, but the idea remains as a possibility for an amusement park proprietor.

The Report of the Royal Commission on London Traffic, published in 1905, records evidence given by C. S. Meik, a civil engineer, in which he suggested new "main avenues" through London 160 ft. wide with suspended railways above the upper deck. Citing the example of the Barmen–Elberfeld Railway, with which we shall be dealing shortly, he stressed the safety of such railways.

The platforms of the suspended railways would have been 16–18 ft. above the level of the upper deck of the main avenue, which deck would carry all the pedestrian traffic. He estimated the cost of the railways at £75,000 a mile.

Giving evidence before the same Royal Commission was F. B. Behr, who figured prominently in the chapter on monorails. He said that an overhead railway could be built on different systems at from £25,000 to £220,000 a mile. He had designed a monorail on much the same route as was authorised for the North Metropolitan Railway & Canal Company, a scheme not pursued because the necessary capital could not be raised. That company had bought the Regent's Canal and designed a railway to run from Paddington to the Victoria & Albert Docks. Behr requested the company to allow him to build an overhead line on his system in practically the same position. He was told informally that they would let him have a right-of-way on reasonable terms. He proposed to use part of the towing path, part of the surplus land, and occasionally to run over the canal itself.

The main line was to have a length of 12 miles 1 furlong. Three branches would bring the total length to 17 miles 6 furlongs 8 chains of double track monorail. From Royal Oak the line would run through St. Johns Wood and thence along the Regent's Canal to Victoria Park. From there it would run along the Hertford Canal, along the Northern Outfall Sewer to Beckton Road, and to the Victoria & Albert Docks. The line would be almost entirely overground, but tunnels for three-quarters of a mile would be needed. The line was intended primarily for passengers and would use the same system as that proposed for the Manchester-Liverpool line. The branches would be from Paddington to Willesden Junction, Haggerston to Broad Street (over the North London Railway), and a further branch over the Regent's Canal to Commercial Docks.

Behr had also designed a monorail from Westminster to Putney Bridge Station over the Chelsea Embankment to cost an estimated £50,000.

The North Metropolitan scheme of 1882 was underground and would have cost £6,000,000 compared with £1,200,000, or £2,000,000 with rolling stock, for the Behr scheme. This latter figure would have included payments to the canal and the North London Railway for the right-of-way.

Only his monorail system, said Behr, would enable the railway to follow the sharp curves of the canal. Switching at the ends of the lines would be avoided by the use of loops. The line would have had some twenty stations and have included gradients in a few places of 1 in 20. Many of the curves would have had radii of between 62 and 100 ft. An average speed of 20 m.p.h. was envisaged with trains of some 50 tons weight. The two main tunnels would have been at Aberdeen Place and Islington and there would have been four other smaller tunnels. Behr estimated that 59,000,000 passengers a year would use his line and the branches and the gross receipts would be more than £500,000.

Meanwhile, in Germany, the suspended monorail was coming to full birth. In the valley of the River Wupper, despite railways on both northern and southern slopes of the valley and a horse tramway, traffic between the towns of Barmen and Elberfeld was becoming congested. A Cologne engineer, Eugen Langen, had come forward with a suggestion for overhead railways and an experimental track was demonstrated at Cologne-Deutz. This seems to have employed a double line with the trolleys running on four wheels on two rails, but it was seen by the engineering advisers of Barmen and Elberfeld and reported on favourably. This experimental track was built by the Continentale Gesellschaft für Elektrische Unternehmungen of Nuremberg, to which organisation Langen sold his rights in 1895.

Plans already submitted by Siemens & Halske for an elevated railway of conventional type were rejected and a contract for the experimental system was drawn up—still using the double rail. Further experiments showed that the double track was less suitable than a monorail, and it was shown that speed could be doubled and the motion of the cars made smoother by using the monorail, largely because it made higher speeds possible round curves. The two towns agreed to its use and work began in 1898. Langen himself never saw his railway, for he had died in October 1895.

Work advanced at such speed that tests were able to be carried out in 1899, and on 1 March 1901, the railway began operation between the Zoologischer Garten station and Kluse, a distance of some $2\frac{3}{4}$ miles. Turning loops were built at the temporary terminals. The section from the Zoo to the permanent terminus at Vohwinkel, 1·9 miles, was opened on 23 May of the same year. This portion of the line leaves the river over which most of the track runs and follows a main street. Work continued from Kruse in the other direction, following the course of the river, and on 27 June 1903 the $3\frac{1}{2}$-mile section to Oberbarmen was opened to traffic, completing the 8·2-mile line. Some 19,200 tons of steel were used in the work, including the stations, and the total cost of construction, including the rolling stock, was 16,000,000 marks. Allowing for the double track, this is about 1,000,000 marks per mile compared with the then cost of 4,000,000 to 6,000,000 marks for an underground railway or 2,700,000 marks for an elevated railway of conventional type.

The cars were designed by Zypen & Charlier, Köln-Deutz—the name was later changed to the familiar Westwaggon—and were all-steel, an innovation in railway construction. The railway started operation with 26 cars, each with two 25-kW motors. In 1903 a further 24 cars were added and in 1912 six more. A new design, of which two cars were built, was introduced in 1930 with two 35-kW motors. There was a high whining noise from the transmission and in an endeavour to eradicate this one car was fitted in 1941 with worm drive; the car had two 65-kW motors. The drive proved so effective that when 20 new cars were obtained from Westwaggon in 1950 they all had worm drive. The new cars had two 45-kW motors. These cars had a weight of 11 tons compared with the 13 tons of the previous cars. The earlier cars had 25 seats and standing room for 40, but the saving in weight with the 1950 cars enabled 31 seats and 49 standing places to be provided.

The cars can be operated individually, but normally two cars form a train. The cars are suspended from two tandem two-wheel bogies connected by yokes to the cars. The current supply is at 600 V. d.c. Signalling is by automatic signals operated by the trains themselves on a station-to-station block system. In case of emergency a telephone is provided on each train so that the station in front or rear can be contacted if necessary.

The train brakes are worked by compressed air obtained from steel tubes below the cars. The tubes are filled at the terminals to a pressure of 150 lb. p.s.i. The brakes work on 65 lb. p.s.i. There is also a handbrake. At peak hours the line is operated on a three-minute headway and the length of the line is covered in 32 minutes; the average travelling speed is 25 km./h., just over 15 m.p.h. During the rest of the day trains run at intervals of 10-12 minutes. The highest permissible speed on the line is 25 m.p.h. and the shortest possible headway is about $1\frac{3}{4}$ minutes.

During the second world war the line was severely damaged by air raids and could be kept going only in sections. The heavy air raids of 30 May and 25 June 1943 put the line completely out of commission. However, by Easter 1946 it was once again open throughout its length. The damage to the superstructure, and the strains to which it had been subjected, were among the reasons for the introduction of the lightweight stock mentioned previously.

The line has a remarkable record for safety. The deep flanges on the bogie wheels effectively prevent derailment. By end of 1954 more than 800,000,000 passengers had been carried and the trains had run 150,000,000 km. Only one passenger was killed in all this travel, and that through the passenger's own carelessness. Rain, snow, and fog have no effect on the running of this line, and, as may be imagined, the town of Wuppertal (into which the twin towns of Barmen and Elberfeld were amalgamated in 1929) is very proud of this unique transport system, the "Schwebebahn".

The platforms at the 18 stations (there were at one time 20) can be either at the sides or in the centre of the tracks. Because the cars are suspended, these platforms do not have to be so far above the ground as in a normal elevated railway and thus passengers have a relatively small number of stairs to climb. Points are ingeniously contrived to make it possible for the trains to be switched on to sidings without needing a break in the continuity of the main line itself. The principle is that the switch tongues form an inclined plane which lifts wheels and flanges of the cars clear of the main line and enables them to pass over it. There are semi-circular loops of about 26 ft. diameter at each end of the track to allow trains to turn round, and there is an additional reversing loop at the Zoologischer Garten station. A large car shed at Vohwinkel has eight roads partially connected by loops.

The colour-light signals are lighted only as the trains approach—possibly one of the first applications of approach-lighted signals—and control automatic blocks extending from station to station. These are an average of 765 yd. apart. The original system was designed by

an engineer named F. Natalis and was built by the
Schuckert Electrical Works, Nuremberg. A number of
modifications have been made from time to time, but
the Natalis principle has been retained. There is a
starting signal at each station which shows red or green.
There is also a yellow signal beside the red "stop" light
which can be illuminated if for any reason a train is to
proceed at "caution" to the station in advance. The
whole of the control apparatus, with its relays, hand
control switches, and pilot lights, is grouped in the
stationmaster's office and can thus be kept under
observation. The stationmaster is also responsible for
action necessary if the automatic signals should fail. He
can keep a signal at red in emergency, irrespective of the
automatic control by trains.

To put into perspective the next overhead development, a British one on the lines of the Schwebebahn but
designed for high speeds, we must go back a number of
years. A German scientist who had been engaged on
work on airship propellers in the first world war suggested in 1918 that the motive power of the German
railways might be supplemented by fitting airship and
aircraft engines, no longer required now that the war
was over, to railway vehicles. These would be driven by
an aircraft propeller and, he thought, should reach high
speeds. His idea was turned down but Dr. Otto
Steinitz continued to advocate it and eventually a trial
car was built. Steinitz proposed a light car with ball
bearings but he had to put up with a heavy car on conventional lines. His fight for a streamline shape also
failed.

Despite the failure of the builders to appreciate
the need for any but orthodox methods of construction,
the car, with a powerful aero engine driving a propeller
at one end, worked very well and made a successful
trial run in May 1919. It also hauled a very heavy and

(*Above*) Louis XIV's pleasure "railway" at Marly-le-Roi.

(*Below*) Gerard's "chemin de fer glissant" in his park at La Jonchère.

(*Photos: courtesy of W. G. F. Roberts Es*

The Brighton - Rottingdean "Daddy Longlegs" car approaching terminus at high water

"Daddy Longlegs" car; line uncovere at low tide.

(*Below*)   London Post Office Railway car.

(*Photo: General Post Offic*

unsuitable trailer car. Then for a year this car, designed for long high-speed runs, acted as a shunting and transfer locomotive in the freight yards of Berlin—work for which it was entirely uneconomic. Not surprisingly, it faded into obscurity.

The work of Steinitz was not lost, however, for it was taken up by Herr Kruckenburg in 1930. He fitted an oil engine of 600 h.p., driving a propeller, to a specially designed 28-ton passenger coach and achieved a speed of 140 m.p.h. As it used conventional railway track, we regret that the career of this remarkable coach has no further place in this book.

The British invention was that of George Bennie, who combined the Wuppertal ideas with those of Steinitz and demonstrated at the meeting of the British Association in 1928 a large-scale model of a suspended monorail system in which a light coach, shaped rather like a torpedo, was driven by airscrews mounted at both ends. By the following year a full-size car had been built. Work commenced on a test section of track over a disused spur of the London & North Eastern Railway outside Milngavie, near Glasgow, and in July 1930 the 426-ft. length of track was in service. In October of that year, Bennie announced that the Blackpool Corporation would support a Bill for the first stage, across the River Ribble, of a Bennie line running from Fleetwood to Blackpool and on *via* Kirkham, Hundred End, Southport and Liverpool to Manchester. A company was also formed to build a 30 km. line in France. Regrettably, as with so many of these schemes, the plans came to nothing.

A pamphlet was issued in 1935 by Inter-Counties Limited which gave full particulars of what had come to be known as "The Railplane System of Transport".

The streamline car was suspended from bogies running on a single overhead rail and was driven by airscrews turned by oil engines or electric motors as desired. The track, a lattice box girder in form, was supported at the required height by steel trestles spaced at 80-ft. intervals and requiring only the small pieces of ground taken for their foundations. The main rail was fixed below the lattice girder and a lighter structure beneath carried an auxiliary rail which controlled the sway of the car. A walkway for inspection ran inside the lattice girder.

The cars tended to swing on curves and take up a natural degree of "bank", but the wheels of the bogies had deep flanges and the clearance of the car mounting below the track was such that even though the car might tend to lift at high speeds it could not rise sufficiently to take the flanges clear of the track. The system was thus absolutely safe.

There are no sudden loads on motors driving air-screws, but when these are electrically driven careful design is needed to take advantage of the extra power obtainable for short periods from electric motors. The design of the propellers of the railplane was a special feature. It was claimed that speeds of 200 m.p.h. could be obtained and maintained with economy.

The guide wheels which engaged with the lower rail were fitted side-by-side in pairs, with vertical axles. The braking system did not act on the wheels of the bogies, but on the rails. One brake shoe gripped the top rail and the other the bottom. The brakes could be worked by the driver and the signalling system and could be set, by adjusting the springs controlling their pressure on the rails, to give a braking effect equal to that of a London bus. This was about four times the rate allowed in normal railway practice.

The cars could be arranged to seat 50 to 100 passengers and could run singly or as a multiple-unit train controlled by a single driver. When running as a train the cars could be coupled by a clever device which, though flexible, revolved at a speed equal to that of the airscrews. There was an ingenious system of signalling which could also control the trains if necessary.

The usual red, yellow, and green signals along the track itself were reproduced on a board before the driver in his cab. If a yellow (caution) light was ignored it would change to red and also automatically apply the brakes, bringing the train to a stand. The airscrews, however, continued to revolve, so that when the light changed to green the brakes were released and the car started forward again. Thus the trains could run in any conditions of weather or visibility. In normal running the driver could also use the propellers, working in reverse, as additional braking.

The trial car at Milngavie was built by Arrol-Johnstone & Aster, Dumfries, except for the ends and the bogies. These were constructed by Mirlees Watson, Glasgow. The specially designed motors, each giving 60 b.h.p. at 1,200 r.p.m. and capable of an output of 240 b.h.p. at 1,800 r.p.m. for short bursts, were built by Laurence Scott & Electromotors, Norwich. The airscrews were designed by Airscrews Limited, Weybridge, and the special signalling by Tyer & Company. The steelwork of the track was fabricated by the Teesside Bridge & Engineering Co. Ltd., Middlesbrough.

A feature of the construction was that any small obstructions such as roads, streams, and conventional railways could be crossed by the normal trackwork, and even where bigger obstructions were encountered the trains were so light that no heavy engineering work was required—a light structure would suffice. Except for the footings for the trackwork no earthworks were required, and as the trains could negotiate gradients of up to 1 in 25 most irregularities of ground could be overcome by varying the length of the supports.

Several suggestions of interest were made for the em-

ployment of the Bennie Railplane, including a London–
Paris route using a railplane from London to Folkestone, ship or seaplane from Folkestone to Boulogne,
and a railplane from Boulogne to Paris. It was estimated
that the 269 miles would be covered in $2\frac{1}{2}$ hours using a
seaplane and $3\frac{1}{2}$ hours using a ship for the Channel
crossing. Another proposal was a line, partly over the
main line of the then Great Western Railway, to Heston,
which at that time was used as the airport for London.
Earlier suggestions had been made for a line to Croydon
when aircraft for London landed there. The proposal to
use the space over existing railways and thus separate
fast from slow traffic is reminiscent of the suggestions
put forward by Behr for his high-speed Manchester–
Liverpool monorailway. Finally, there was a scheme
for linking satellite towns near Waltham Abbey and
Dagenham by a line following the route of the River
Lea and the Northern Outfall Sewer.

After remaining, forlorn, for some years at Milngavie, the car and test track were dismantled and sold
in 1956.

In 1952 there was a proposal for a 44-mile monorail
on the Wuppertal principle between San Fernando and
a terminal near the Union station in Los Angeles in the
U.S.A. Arch-shaped supports were proposed which
would straddle the Los Angeles River for some distance
and then the line would be carried along the river bank
on V-shaped supports. It was estimated that the 15
miles between the densely-populated suburb of Van
Nuys and Los Angeles would be covered in 28 minutes
including nine intermediate stops. This compares with
a time of 63 minutes for the bus journey. Towers 35 ft.
high and spanning 75 ft. would be spaced at intervals of
33 ft. The towers would probably be of concrete to con-
serve steel and reduce cost. The proposed cars would
hang from two-wheel bogies running on 100 lb. rails,

and would carry 60 seated and 40 standing passengers. Other schemes have been considered by San Francisco, where a line to the densely-populated area on the opposite side of San Francisco Bay is mooted, and by Sacramento where a four-mile line to a residential area is under discussion.

In mid-1956 the Tokyo Transportation Bureau was reported to be considering the construction of a high-speed monorail system to cope with increasing congestion in the city.

The last full-size monorail to be built is at Houston, Texas, where a pilot test line has been built at Arrowhead Park, on the old Spanish Trail. Work started on 20 August 1955, and the 970-ft. line was opened on 18 February 1956. The cost was some $120,000. The coach is suspended in a similar fashion to the Wuppertal and Bennie coaches from eight pneumatic-tyred wheels.

The line can run at ground level, suspended overhead, or underground, and Monorail Inc., the sponsors of the system, which has been named the "Skyway" line, claim that any speed up to 250 m.p.h. is possible. The towers were designed in an inverted "J" shape so that they can stand at the side of a street and cantilever the actual line out over the centre of the road. The height can be anything within reason—those on the trial line vary from 30 to 10 ft. They can be built to bring the coach down to ground level for loading at stations. The rail itself is of steel pipe on top of which ride the wheels and the power equipment.

The coach employs a new principle of construction called "concentric suspension" for the frame. It can run in either direction and the driver, who sits in a cab on top of the rail, can turn his seat to face either way. The trial coach, known as the "Trailblazer", is 55 ft. in length, but coaches can be made longer or shorter as required. The height is 7 ft. and the inside width is 8 ft.

There are 60 seats and room for some 50 standing passengers. The fibreglass skin of the coach covers 3,000 sq. ft. The seats are arranged in a diagonal pattern, an idea borrowed from the buses of Stockholm, Sweden, which allows greater space for passengers. Four doors allow the coach to be emptied or filled in 30 seconds. The two 305-h.p. internal combustion engines fitted are said to allow a speed of 100 m.p.h. but this could be greatly increased with higher power.

There are automatic electric brakes and couplings and mechanical brakes are provided for emergencies. The coach is air-conditioned. The engines drive through gears and two speeds are available. The tyres lock on the rail and on top of the rail proper is a locking guide rail. There are eight auxiliary wheels which come into play if a tyre should burst.

After eight months of tests the sponsors announced that a new design had been evolved suitable for areas with low-density populations. A 1,250-ft. line to this design has been built at the Autorama in Hypoluxo, Florida, near Fort Lauderdale. This is some 27 ft. high and uses a 26-passenger coach. This railway was completed by the end of 1956 at a cost of $75,000. An example of the original heavy-density line is being built at the State Fair of Texas, and many of the materials from the Houston line, including the original coach, are being used in it. Two new coaches are also to be used. The low-density line costs some $300,000 a mile and the heavy-density some $500,000.

With the completion of the Hypoluxo line, an application is to be made for authority to build and operate a Skyway monorail to connect Miami, Miami Beach, Fort Lauderdale, and the Palm Beaches.

The last system to be considered in detail is a British/ French design for a suspended line which came into prominence when an improved link to London Airport was under consideration. It is sponsored by International Monorail Limited. Although it is called a monorail design, the cars actually run on four-wheel bogies fitted with pneumatic tyres. The bogies travel inside a large box girder which is split to allow the supports for the cars to pass through. The bogies are "steered" inside the girder by four horizontal guide wheels, also fitted with pneumatic tyres, which are pressed against the inside walls of the girder. The twin girders, for two-way traffic, can be supported by a T-shaped structure at intervals or by gantries when a centre support is impracticable. Placing the bogies and their electric motors inside the girder protects them from the weather and also reduces noise appreciably. The electrical conductors are also inside the girder and are mounted under the top surface. The airport line cars are designed on aircraft principles and resemble aircraft without wings or tail. They seat 60 and have full luggage accommodation. A maximum speed of 75 m.p.h. is envisaged with starting acceleration at 3·83 ft. per second. The cars can run singly or in trains. Each car is suspended from its twin bogies by articulated links which allow it to swing outward on curves but undue swinging is prevented by damping apparatus.

Each bogie has two electric motors held in an H–form frame to which the running and guide wheels are also attached, the latter on front and rear extensions. The spring supports for the pantographs are carried on the bogies. The primary suspension is of rubber units which isolate the bogie frame from the axles. It absorbs sudden longitudinal stresses, gives an elastic reaction to the motor coupling, and balances the over-run of the motor.

The car rides smoothly on the pneumatic tyres and the actual suspension from the bogie has been given variable flexibility. This has been done by the action of an elastic thrust acting progressively in parallel with the central helical spring. Pivoting is by a rubber ring resting on the central spring by means of a slide. A stabilising bar on top of the car reduces lateral rolling.

The running wheels of the bogie are standard Michelin Metallic lorry wheels with a diameter, under load, of 3 ft. 2 in. to 3 ft. 4 in. The inner tubes are filled with nitrogen to reduce fire risks if the tyre should become overheated. The lateral guide wheels would also be inflated with nitrogen and be of 2 ft. 4 in. dia. The wheels would be fitted with roller bearings.

For the London Airport line, where no intermediate stations were envisaged, it was considered that hydraulic servo brakes would suffice, and a master cylinder is provided on each bogie. A handbrake would suffice for parking. The transmission from motors to axles is a double reduction type employing a motor-vehicle-type differential. The London Airport line cars would have two 120 h.p. motors to each bogie, giving 480 h.p. to each car. Direct current at 650 or 750 V. would be used.

The cars would be of stainless Austenitic steel shot welded on the Budd system, giving an external appearance of unpainted rustless metal. There would be a driver's cab at the front with the main passenger compartment in the centre and a luggage compartment at the rear. The passenger compartment would have four doors and be provided, in one design, with 60 aluminium frame seats. These would be arranged with two seats on one side of the gangway and one on the other with a change of the single and double seats to the opposite sides halfway down the car to maintain balance. There would be large glazed windows with luggage racks above them. The luggage compartment would have large folding doors on each side, and would accommodate two four-wheel trolleys fitted with racks to take the luggage. Loading and unloading the complete trolleys would save a great deal of time at terminals and enable the cars to be used more intensively. The car would be fitted with a type of air conditioning.

On straight sections the box girders would be supported on T-supports at 100-ft. intervals, standing on a centre reservation in the road. The girder itself would be built up of welded steel plates with reinforcement on the under, or running, side. It would be welded continuously in 1,000-ft. lengths necessitating expansion joints of an ingenious design. Points are arranged by having a movable section of the box girder resting at one end on the fixed track which it joins and at the other on a pivot. The section is also suspended from a cradle running on rails set in the segment of a circle. The cradle is electrically driven to move the point section to an angle of 6 deg. with the straight portion. These points must be taken at low speed but are needed only for the selection of terminal platforms and at the car sheds. At the terminals the single-ended cars, which can run in tandem, are turned by loops.

Automatic block signalling with colour lights would be used, the signals being operated by track circuits. One wall of the box girder would be insulated for this purpose. The signals could be repeated in the drivers' cabs.

Although the system has a long history of development, the recent phases began with a design by Mr. Hugh Fraser, a Scottish engineer. International Monorail was formed by Railplanes Limited and the Société Lyonnaise des Eaux et de l'Eclairage, Paris. The improved designs were developed in conjunction with Messrs. Hitchins, Jervis, and Partners, Consulting Engineers, Westminster.

A model of the system, in full working order, was shown at the Science Museum in London on 30 and 31 May 1956, and has subsequently been shown elsewhere in Britain. It is planned to show the model in Cuba and North America.

CHAPTER TEN

CONCRETE TRACKS

THE use of concrete for railway tracks in various forms has been mentioned in other chapters of this book, but there are one or two roadbeds using concrete in so essential a form as to be worthy of a short chapter to themselves.

The first of these was installed in the Kathiawar Peninsula in Western India, near Khambalia. This experimental line, nine miles in length, was a concrete track carrying pneumatic-tyred passenger and goods vehicles. It was 3 ft. wide and between six and nine inches in depth. The vehicles were kept to this narrow track by a central guide rail.

The line, if we can call the track that, was built on a roadbed 7 ft. wide on embankments and in cuttings, and needed bridges four feet in width. Although the line was laid purely as an experiment it served a useful purpose and showed a profit on the capital outlay. In 1935, the line was examined by the Government of India and the Government of Bombay and pronounced suitable for carrying goods and passengers. It was accordingly given the status of registration under the appropriate Transport Act.

The system is known as the "Guideways" system, and is said to be cheap both in prime cost and in upkeep. There are no sleepers, and the single rail, spiked into the concrete, need not be heavy in section. As it serves only as a guide, it bears no load and can be of secondhand material. The only normal maintenance required is the occasional sweeping of sand and stones from the track.

The rolling stock can be used on ordinary roads as well as on the special track, so that delivery to the premises of a consignee, or collection, presents no difficulties.

The vehicles used were 7 ft. in width—hence the total roadbed width of 7 ft.—and had a gauge between the centres of the pneumatic wheels of 2 ft. These dimensions approximate closely to those of the 2-ft. gauge railways of India. The stock used on the trial line had to be rather higher than was desirable because the only pneumatic tyres available there at the time the line was built had a diameter of 2 ft. 6 in. In fact, the extra height was found not to affect stability, and the larger wagons, which had 12-wheel bogies, were given a central well which brought the load lower and improved stability.

Burst tyres were no problem. The remaining five wheels of the six-wheeled vehicles and the similar number of wheels on the bogies of the bogie vehicles were ample to support the load even when wagons were loaded to full capacity. A tyre actually burst on a trial run only a mile from the start, but the train carried on quite happily to the end of its journey. Special tyres were ordered later from the Dunlop Rubber Co. Ltd.

The locomotive and vehicles were guided by rollers fixed at the front and rear which ran on each side of the guide rail and thus kept them to the proper track. The tractive effort provided by the rubber tyres enabled greater loads to be hauled for a given locomotive axle loading and steeper gradients to be negotiated than is the case on orthodox railways.

The diesel locomotive used on the Khambalia line weighed 4 tons and had eight pneumatic tyres. The track and rolling stock were designed by Mr. Clifford Skelton, a retired railway engineer.

The idea was taken up by J. Brockhouse & Co. Ltd. and the Executive Engineer of the Company, Mr. R. E.

Hagley, produced designs for a locomotive, vehicles, and track. The system was called the "Uniline" and a demonstration was given at Mayfield in Sussex, where the experimental track was built, on 6 April 1951. The track, as in the Indian trials, was some 3 ft. wide and the stock had a similar guiding system with vertical rollers at front and rear. All vehicles were fitted with pneumatic tyres. In the course of the demonstration on the half-mile track loads of 21 tons were hauled up a gradient of 1 in 15 at a speed of $4\frac{1}{2}$ m.p.h.

Drawings lent to us by J. Brockhouse & Co. Ltd. show the locomotive used to have been, in railway parlance, a 2-4-2 with a 90-b.h.p. 4-cyl. diesel engine. It was 15 ft. 9 in. over the buffers, which were single and central, and the wheelbase was 10 ft.; the leading and trailing wheels had tyres 24 in. $\times 7$ in. and the driving-wheel tyres were 27 in. $\times 7$ in. There were four guide roller sets arranged in pairs in front of and behind the leading and trailing wheels. The total weight in working order was 5 tons.

The primary gearbox was a Meadow's type 10 4-speed box with clutch and provision for power take-off. It was not fitted with a reverse gear. The secondary gearbox was a "Brockhouse" single speed and reverse gearbox provided with a jackshaft and coupling rod final drive. The two gearboxes were connected by a flexible coupling. All tyres were inflated at a pressure of 90 lb. p.s.i. The locomotive was designed to take curves of 50-ft. radius. Compensated brakes were fitted to each axle and an air compressor, reservoir, and driver's brake valve were provided to allow continuous automatic brakes to be used on the train vehicles.

The drawings show 3-ton vehicles with four wheels, $4\frac{1}{2}$-ton vehicles with six, 6-ton vehicles with eight, and 10-ton vehicles with two six-wheel bogies. The calculated performance figures with the locomotive mentioned showed that up to 25 m.p.h. might be attained with a suitable load and in first gear a load of 126 tons might be hauled on the level. Mr. Hagley said at the demonstration that the system had not been designed to compete with existing road or rail transport systems, but to supplement them. It appears to have considerable possibilities, particularly in undeveloped countries.

A rail-guided, partially road-borne railway on the Ewing system operated in the State of Patiala in India for many years. The road surface may not have been concrete but the system belongs to this chapter, if only because it could well be used with modern concrete roads. The line was built by Marsland Price & Company of Bombay. As in the Uniline arrangement, there was a single rail, but instead of being straddled by the vehicles it bore the wheels on one side of them. The wheels were double-flanged to keep them on the rail. The vehicles had at least two of these wheels on the rail to give fore-and-aft stability and were stabilised sideways by a wheel borne on the end of an arm and running on the surface of the roadway beside which the single rail was laid. The effect was rather like that of a motorcycle and sidecar, with the cycle wheels running on the rail and the sidecar wheels running on the roadway and maintaining balance. At points, a whole section of rail was moved into place between the tracks to be joined. The double flanges of the wheel made this method essential. The balance wheels were smooth and wide and rode easily over even poor roads. There were both goods and passenger vehicles, some even being fitted with bogies and carrying about six tons. There were steam and petrol locomotives, but animal power was also used. In all, some 55 miles of line were authorised on this system.

A guide-rail system still in use, and in which the vehicles are borne on road wheels, is to be found in, of all unlikely places, a tunnel running between the Senate Office and the Capitol in Washington. The cars look rather like miniature open trams with poles reaching up to collect current from and return it to overhead conductor rails. The "trams" hold a dozen passengers. There are no doors, and as the line is in a subway no roof was thought necessary.

We have been saving one of the most important concrete track systems until the end, but before we go on to describe it we must mention that a very remarkable idea was produced 25 years ago or so in Russia. The inventor proposed electric trains running in concrete troughs on balls instead of wheels, and a photograph we have seen of a model makes it look very workmanlike. Unfortunately, we have not been able to glean any details of the system, but we understand that it promised very high speeds.

The Alweg system of transport is, in its broader aspects, the conception of Dr. Axel L. Wenner-Gren, a Swedish-born international industrialist. It was first shown at Fühlingen, near Cologne in Germany, on 8 October 1952, when a demonstration model on a scale of 1:2·5 was demonstrated to guests. A group to study transport problems was formed, called the "Verkehrsbahnen-Studiengesellschaft", and this group was re-formed in January 1953 as "Alweg-Forschung G.m.b.H."

The Alweg trains run on a track made up of a continuous reinforced concrete beam, known as the "beamway". The beams are hollow, to save weight, and are carried on reinforced concrete pylons 35–45 ft. apart. The height depends on the country over which the line passes. In open country it can be only a few feet from the ground and in towns it can be any desired height to allow traffic on roads or conventional railways to pass underneath. The supporting pylons are so shaped and set as to force the train into its correct path on transition curves, a feature having great importance in operation of the trains at high speeds.

The body of the train is of light metal, and each vehicle is carried on two bogies. The whole shape is aerodynamic and the beamway and supports, where they are near the train level, are also shaped aerodynamically. The cars ride on the top of the beams but have extensions to the sides which come down on each side of the beams. It is intended that in full-size trains the baggage compartments, kitchens, toilets, and so on shall be in these side extensions and thus help to lower the centre of gravity. Separate doors at a lower level will give access to these lower compartments, so that by using two-level platforms at stations it will be possible to load luggage, take on restaurant car supplies, and service the train without interference with passenger circulation on the upper platform.

Freight trains will be of similar design, except for tank cars, which, because of the density of their loads, will be narrower than the standard. Bulk cargoes will be loaded through the roof and unloaded through doors in the bottom of the side extensions. Cargoes such as coal or ore can be loaded mechanically from above and will discharge themselves by gravity through the bottom doors.

The propulsive force required by the train is low and because of this it is possible to attain very high speeds economically. A cruising speed of 200 m.p.h. should be possible in the full-size train.

The test train is some 60 ft. in length and has a diameter of 5 ft. with the extensions downwards; the vertical height is 6 ft. 6 in. It has three cars, articulated, each of which is carried on two bogies. The bogies themselves are divided into a carrying saddle and a stabilising saddle. The forces set up by the train are transferred to the beam by individual cylindrical wheels so arranged that no wheel transfers forces working in the direction of its axle. The design ensures also that no force can act on wheels other than those intended for it.

There are three factors concerned in the movement of the train: carrying forces, guiding forces, and tilting forces. These are assigned respectively to the carrying wheels, the guiding wheels of the carrying saddle, and the stabilising wheels of the stabilising saddle.

The carrying forces work on the carrying saddle through a spring element and pass through the stabilising axis to it, the stabilising saddle being set outside the carrying saddle over a segment bearing. Because the carrying forces pass through this they exercise no turning effect on the stabilising wheels. The carrying saddle therefore cannot tilt to any significant degree and is thus always in the best position to transfer carrying forces to the main wheels efficiently.

The lateral forces which arise when the beam causes the train to change its direction of travel are transferred from the carrying saddle to the beam by the guiding wheels. There is a certain amount of play, strictly controlled by strong springs, which takes up any inaccuracies in the beam. Any tilting forces arising from wind pressure or uneven loading are transferred to the stabilising saddle through transition guide elements. This force is taken by the stabilising wheels, which are spring-mounted, and transferred to the beam quite independently of carrying and guiding forces.

The beam has a prepared track on its narrow top surface for the carrying wheels, tracks at the top and bottom edges of the broad side for the side thrust wheels (guiding and stabilising), and rails mounted on insulators at the foot of the beam which serve as pick-up rails for the electrical power. The train is also fitted with normal flanged wheels and if desired can run from the beamway on to ordinary railway track, on which it can run at reduced, but still high, speed.

The Alweg train can surmount gradients of 1 in 7 and fewer earthworks are therefore required to prepare a track for it. Small undulations of the country over which it runs can be taken care of by varying the lengths of the supports. The train would obviously be very difficult to derail, and all trains running can be controlled by a special automatic train control system. On the train, only an attendant to monitor the system is required. No details of this system have been released, but it is understood that it will not require extensive use of conduits and mechanical controls, and no visual signals will be required on the line itself. In addition to this control system, an emergency headway control will be provided which will prevent trains approaching each other too closely. It is claimed that it will be possible to have very short headways with the system—much shorter than can be obtained with the normal block system.

The Alweg train is conceived as part of a complete transport system which includes methods of train classification and assembly, terminal clearance, delivery from terminal to consignee, bulk cargo handling, waybill processing, ticket issuing, and so on.

The points used on the Alweg track are massive, consisting of two sections of track to give the required connections mounted on a sliding base. The whole section is moved sideways as required to bring the desired piece of track into alignment.

On 1 January 1957, it was announced from Cologne that the Alweg Monorail Corporation (Bahamas) had been awarded a contract to rebuild the entire public transport of the city of São Paulo, Brazil, on the Alweg system, a contract valued at £55,000,000. On 12 February 1957 the Minister of Lands & Forests for

British Columbia announced that an "agreement of intent" had been entered into between the British Columbia Government and the Axel Wenner-Gren interests. The agreement was in respect of a project which would include the building of a high-speed monorail line to span the gap between the Pacific Great Eastern Railway, running from Prince George, and the northern boundary of British Columbia. Construction was expected to start in 1960.

CHAPTER ELEVEN

SOME OTHER SYSTEMS

A N application of magnetism to railway traction was made by Bachelet, a French engineer who designed a system which he thought would enable tremendous speeds to be obtained. He dispensed with any form of rails, and almost with any form of track, but along the route he proposed to have a series of huge electromagnets, or, to be more precise, solenoids, for they were in the form of huge rings through which the cars of the railway—if we can call it that—would pass. The basis of the system was the fact that magnetism repels certain metals and attracts others. The car was to be lifted from the ground at the terminal station by repulsion magnets. Once off the ground, it was drawn forward by the ring magnets. As speed mounted, the repulsion magnets became more widely spaced and at top speed the ring magnets were enough to keep the car in the air and also draw it forward. There was no friction, except that of air, so speeds of at least 300 m.p.h. were thought possible.

A model of the system was built and worked, but it got no further than that.

One of the most fantastic of the many traction ideas of the 1840s was that of Parkins. In his system power was supplied by huge windmills with horizontal sails and transmitted by a rope which first passed round a wheel fitted on a platform extending from a coach or on a separate wagon. It was then carried over the coaches by pulleys on the roof, and the end was attached to a shaft. The wheel could be used as a brake. To assist when there was little or no wind, the line was to be laid out as a switchback.

An American named Ezra Coleman anticipated the Wembley Never-Stop Railway by some 80 years. His system fitted trains with a pair of inner wheels which were normally idle. When a steep incline was reached, these wheels ran on to an extra set of inner rails. The contact brought into use a powered endless screw which ran over revolving rollers and acted, through a differential, on the axle of the train, giving it power to surmount the slope.

The first of the Never-Stop Railways, invented and designed by B. R. Adkins and W. Y. Lewis, was laid down at Southend in 1923 and the second at Wembley in 1924 and 1925.

The Southend line was 1,000 ft. in length and that at Wembley was 6,600 ft. with 10 stations—six intermediate and two termini at each end. The Southend cars were 10ft. × 5ft. and those at Wembley 20ft. × 6ft. They had eight and 24 seats respectively, with half the space given over to standing passengers.

Millions of people were carried on them without a single accident, stepping on and off the slow-moving cars as they travelled through the stations. These were so designed that there was no gap between the platform and the floors of the cars, which were at the same level. On both railways there were severe curves and gradients, the curves at the termini being far more severe than could be negotiated by an ordinary railway.

These railways worked without drivers, conductors, or signalmen. Despite the comparatively rapid acceleration and deceleration of the cars, travel was smooth, and the absence of normal braking cut out a good deal of the normal wear and tear experienced with railway vehicles and normal track. Travel was also almost noiseless, as the cars had rubber tyres running on concrete

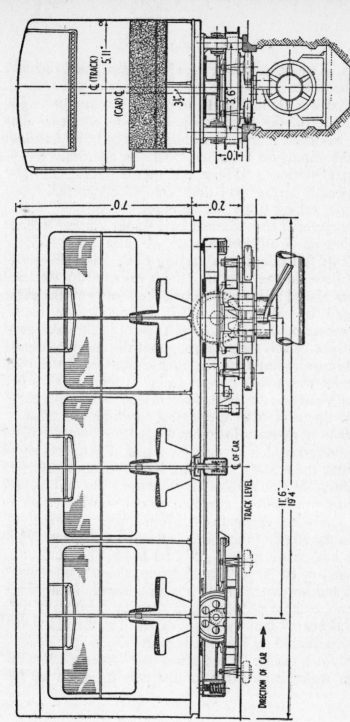

Fig. 6. Car fitted for propulsion by varying pitch spiral drive on the Adkins-Lewis system

tracks, to which they were kept by rubber-tyred horizontal wheels bearing on the inside surfaces of the tracks.

Speed was limited to $1\frac{1}{2}$ m.p.h. at the stations and 12 m.p.h. on the open track, but in recent years the ratio has been increased to allow 1 m.p.h. at stations and 24 m.p.h. on the open track, or alternatively $1\frac{1}{2}$ m.p.h. at stations and 36 m.p.h. on the track. This latter speed is higher than that achieved on normal tube railways, taking stops into account.

The secret of the Adkins-Lewis Rapid Varying Speed Continuous Transport System, to give the "Never-Stop" its full title, is the varying pitch spiral drive located between the tracks. This is revolved by electric motors placed at intervals along the route and the cars engage it by ball-bearing rollers depending from them and embracing the spiral on each side of its thread. They are driven by this means throughout the entire route at speeds corresponding to the pitch between the thread at the point where they happen to be. There can thus be no collisions and although the cars are spaced well apart on the open line they are almost touching at stations.

Screws of all types in common use have, in general, a close uniform pitch engaged by a nut. Friction is high and thus the screw and nut are ideal for joining things together. In the Adkins-Lewis system, the nut is replaced by the rollers, mounted on ball-bearings, which have a very low element of friction. The drive, depending on the angle of the spiral, is thus very efficient. The angle has an average of 45° and has a push-and-pull efficiency of 80–90 per cent in driving the cars up to top speed and lowering it again to station speed. In slowing the cars, a large proportion of their momentum is fed back as energy into the spiral drive. The driving shaft is also mounted on ball-bearings and needs little power to keep it rotating. It is claimed that improvements in design make it possible for the cars to attain up to

36 m.p.h. from station speeds of 1–1½ m.p.h. and that at least 15,000 passengers, seated and standing, could be carried in an hour in 20-ft. long and 6-ft. wide vehicles on a 4-ft. gauge line.

At one of the old Earls Court Exhibitions there was shown a "Dragon Railway", which was very popular with the visitors. The locomotive was built inside a brazen dragon's head and no doubt breathed out appropriate fire and smoke. The passengers sat on seats formed like shelves along the body and the tail of the dragon.

A well-known French engineer, Girard, who carried out much work on turbine development, invented and built a "chemin de fer glissant", or sliding railway. This was built in his park at La Jonchère, probably in the 1880s. Girard's railway had a cast tube running along its length which contained water under high pressure and was supplied from a reservoir. Jets of water sprayed from this at intervals of 100 metres. The cars had no wheels but were fitted with broad flat plates where the wheels would normally have been. These slid along wide cast rails. The action of the water jets produced a thin film of water between the plates and the rails, and the power of the jets also pushed the cars along. The line may be said to represent an opened-out turbine. The system worked and worked well, and was shown at a number of exhibitions, including the Paris Exhibition of 1889. It appears never to have reached a status higher than that of an interesting novelty.

The Scotsman of 28 November 1855 recorded: "For some days past the select committee of the Royal Arsenal at Woolwich has been witnessing the erection of a novel machine invented by a working French engineer, M. Balan, who has obtained a patent from the British Government. The apparatus bears the title of an aerial railway, by which cars and wagons can be propelled by

their own weight on inclined wire ropes. These ropes
are firmly attached at their extremities, and at the ends
where the materials are to be unloaded they are kept
apart by a lever, the length of which varies according to
the inclination required. By means of raising or de-
pressing this lever, the incline of the ropes can be reversed, and the cars or wagons propelled in opposite
directions."

One of the strangest mountain railways ever built
must have been the balloon railway near Salzburg in the
early 1900s. This consisted in essence of a large balloon
tethered to a slide running on a single rail up the mountainside. The connection, by steel cable, allowed the
balloon to float some 35 ft. above the ground.

A car holding ten passengers was suspended from the
balloon. Once loaded, it was allowed to rise up the
slope. To overcome the buoyancy of the balloon and
allow the car to descend again water was allowed to
enter a large tank. The weight of this took the car down
again.

The cable passed through the centre of the balloon car
and the conductor was in charge of a speed regulator—
presumably some form of brake on the slide—which
allowed him to control the speed.

The suggested use of sails on Palmer's railway has
been mentioned in an earlier chapter, but that was not
the only use of this means of propulsion. The single-line
railway at Spurn Head, connecting the small village
of Kilnsea to the Head itself, had a sail-propelled trolley
which was used by the lifeboatmen to reach their vessel.
At one time the local people living on the Thames
Haven branch of the former London, Tilbury &
Southend Railway used a sail-propelled trolley to travel
on the branch. Sails were used in similar fashion on the
Baltimore & Ohio line in the U.S.A. and on the Anto-
fagasta (Chile) & Bolivia Railway.

An ingenious method of propelling light trains or buses has been tried out in Switzerland. This consists of mounting, as far as railways are concerned, a heavy flywheel in a railway vehicle. To reduce friction the wheel is mounted on ball bearings and is enclosed in an airtight box. As with the gyroscopic cars mentioned in an earlier chapter, the ideal would be to take all the air out of the box and create a vacuum. This presents difficulties in practice, and the Oerlikon Company, which is responsible for the trials, found it simpler to fill the box with hydrogen, which gives much less resistance than air to the turning of the wheel.

The flywheel is started and worked up to full speed by an electric motor mounted on the same spindle and also enclosed in the box. Once speed has been attained the current is disconnected and the motor becomes a dynamo. It supplies current to a motor which drives the car for some 10 miles before the energy of the flywheel is exhausted.

By having recharging points *en route* to which the car can be plugged in, the journey can be continued as long as necessary, for it takes only two or three minutes for the flywheel to be brought back to full speed. In this way electric traction can be used without conductor rails or overhead equipment, the only inconvenience being the necessity to stop for a few minutes every 8 – 10 miles.

The first electric railway in the world was laid down for an exhibition in Berlin in 1879. It was the work of Dr. Werner von Siemens. The first public railway to be driven by electricity was also in Berlin, or rather at Lichterfelde, a suburb, and opened in May 1881. The first electric line in Britain was devised by Magnus Volk, Electrical Engineer to the Brighton Corporation, who in August 1883 opened a railway from the Aquarium to the Chain Pier. This line, later extended to Black

Rock, is now owned by the Corporation. Except for its early date, there was nothing particularly unusual about it. The unusualness was in the extension built to Rottingdean.

The Brighton & Rottingdean Seashore Electric Tramroad Company obtained powers in 1893 for this line, and Volk designed a saloon car weighing some 40 tons. It was 50 ft. long and 22 ft. wide and was mounted on long legs. Twenty-four feet below the deck of the car were the wheels, enclosed in "spats", four to each steel leg. These bogies ran on two parallel tracks each of 2 ft 8½ in. gauge, arranged so that the outside rails were 18 ft. apart. The long legs were needed because the track ran along the beach for some 2¾ miles and at high tide the tracks were under 15 ft. of water. Not unnaturally, the car was soon known popularly as "Daddy Long-Legs".

Power for the four 25-h.p. electric motors was drawn from a trolley wire mounted on high posts beside the track, and the wheels were driven by shafts inside the legs. Some 150 passengers could crowd on to this car. In December 1896, only a month after the opening, the line was badly damaged and the car wrecked by a great gale which also destroyed the Chain Pier. A new car was built complete with lifebelts and a boat, and the line restored, starting work again in August 1897. The speed was some 5–6 m.p.h. and a trip on it at high tide was said to give all the pleasure of a sea trip without the rocking. The line was dismantled in 1901 to make way for the lengthening of groins on the foreshore.

The car had two decks with a saloon on the lower deck and a brass plate in the saloon recorded that King Edward VII, when Prince of Wales, rode on this remarkable railway that went to sea.

An ingenious idea for slipping and picking up coaches from a moving train was once devised and a model—

which worked—was built to demonstrate it. The idea was that a train should have a slip coach attached to it and that coach should have an extra set of wheels of a gauge wider than the ordinary track. When the slip station was reached, the outer wheels engaged with a track laid outside (on each side) the ordinary track. The coach remained attached to the train by a wire cable which drew it up a ramp, running on the wide gauge lines. At the top of the ramp was waiting another specially equipped coach with passengers to join the train. The cable was transferred automatically to this second coach which ran down the other side of the ramp as the cable pulled it. On reaching the end of the special track it ran on the ordinary rails, drawn by the train through the cable. As the train went on, the cable was wound in and the coach attached to the train. If the idea had ever been adopted, passengers would have had a very rough time when the coach was jerked from a standstill by the train.

We have not been concerned with ordinary underground railways in this book, but one which must be mentioned is the Post Office (London) Railway. There is nothing very strange about the line and its vehicles, except that they are miniature. It qualifies for inclusion in this book because the trains have no drivers.

In 1909 a Departmental Committee was set up to consider improved methods of carrying mails in London which would avoid delays to road transport caused through fogs, street congestion, and so on. This was reminiscent of the Pneumatic Despatch railway already described. The Committee examined many types of pneumatically and electrically operated railways and finally recommended that an electric tube railway should be built for two-way traffic. The trains, they proposed, should be automatic, and have no drivers.

The recommendation of the committee was accepted

and in 1913 a Select Committee of the House of Lords approved the Post Office (London) Railway Bill which gave effect to the scheme. There were to be eight stations, at Paddington District Office, Western Parcels Office, Western District Office, West Central District Office, Mount Pleasant, King Edward Building, Liverpool Street station, and the Eastern District Office.

A contract was placed for the tunnel work, etc., in 1914 and in the same year a short section of track was erected on Plumstead Marshes for experimental purposes. The first world war held up the work, but the main tunnel was completed and, in fact, was used for storing museum exhibits and so on for safety during the rest of the war.

At the end of the war, prices had risen so much that the electrical work was not proceeded with, and the scheme was revised to make the equipment simpler and less expensive. The new scheme was ready by 1923 and tenders were sent out. Contracts were placed in 1924. Half the line was ready for staff training by May 1927, and the whole line was opened for traffic in December 1927. Today, the railway carries some 6,500,000 letter bags and 4,000,000 parcels bags each year. The bags are placed in containers, of which each car can carry four, and the trains consist of one or two cars.

The line is 6½ miles long and runs in a tunnel about 70 ft. down. Except for sections where it crosses sewers, tube railways, and so on, it is level. The stations vary in distance apart, the shortest being 380 yd. and the longest 1 mile 293 yd. A feature discussed when we dealt with the Kearney system is included, that is that the stations are rather higher than the main tracks so that there is an upward slope into them which decelerates trains, and also a downward slope away from them which helps the trains to gain speed. At stations there are two tunnels side by side connected by horizontal tunnels. The smallest station is 90 ft. long and the largest 313 ft.

The railway track is of 2-ft. gauge and the rails weigh 35 lb. to the yard. There is a central conductor rail of channel-section mild steel which is raised three inches above the running tracks. Both of the running rails are insulated, one being used for the return circuit of the operating current and the other, divided into sections, for track circuiting.

The tunnel is 9 ft. in diameter and the bottom is filled with loose ballast on which is laid a 12-in. concrete raft. In the raft are channels for each track and the sleepers are let into the concrete at 4 ft. 3 in. intervals. The twin station tunnels each have two tracks, one of which, beside the platform, is used for stopping trains, and the other, on the outside, for through trains. The conductor rails carry direct current at 440 V. and this is used for most of the line. Certain low-speed sections, however, are supplied at 150 V.

The automatic control of the trains is achieved through the track circuits already mentioned. A train passing to a new section closes the track circuit on that section. This cuts off the driving current in the section that has just been left. When the train reaches the next section ahead the track circuit of that section turns off the current in the section just left and at the same time turns on the current in the last section but one. Thus there is always a dead section behind each train which protects it. Switch cabins are provided to give control of the more complicated position at stations. A special camshaft apparatus stops all trains just before stations at which they call, and they are then brought into the station at low speed, thus ensuring that they can be stopped exactly where required.

When a train has been sent into a siding the reversing

switches on the cars must be operated by hand before
the train can be brought out again. Special switchgear
ensures that no trains can move on tracks the operator
has to cross and a green light shows him when it is safe
to proceed.   Three stations have sidings at which
three battery locomotives are kept for use when the
current is cut off.

At three of the smaller stations the control of the
trains is entirely automatic, the trains waiting at the
platform approaches until the platform is clear.

The original cars, 90 in number, were run in groups
of three.   Certain disadvantages became apparent in
service, however, and new cars were designed of much
greater capacity. The original cars began to be taken out
of service in 1930 and were completely replaced by May
1931.   The new cars used parts of the old, including
motors and driving wheels, and 50 were built. They had
a capacity equivalent to 150 cars of the old type. Ten
more were added in 1936.

The main body of the present cars holds four containers, and it is supported at each end by motor bogies.
The driving wheels are 24 in. in diameter and the pony
wheels, which are under the main body, are only 12 in.
in diameter. Each driving motor is of 22 b.h.p. The two
collector shoes on each bogie are spaced well apart so
that gaps in the conductor rail are bridged. The current
supplied to the motors also runs through a brake solenoid.   The brakes are normally kept applied to the
wheels by springs. This solenoid overcomes the power
of the springs and takes the brakes off.

The reversing handle has three positions, the outside
positions allowing the car to run backwards or for-
wards. When it is in the centre position current is cut
off and when the brakes have been taken off by a handwheel the car can be moved "dead" by hand or by a
battery locomotive. The lever cannot be moved from

this position until the brakes have applied again by un-screwing the handwheel.

A car depot at Mount Pleasant stores spare cars and also has full maintenance facilities.

At Paddington and Liverpool Street, there are elaborate conveyor systems for carrying mails between the main-line trains and the Post Office Railway.

Under the streets of Chicago is a network of tunnels known to comparatively few people. It started its existence early in this century when the Illinois Tele-phone and Telegraph Company started to build tunnels to carry its wires and cables. The company's money was exhausted after about 20 miles of tunnel had been built and it sold out to the Illinois Tunnel Company, which intended to work freight through the tunnels. Still another company, the Chicago Warehouse & Terminal Company, was formed for the purpose of building tunnels under the city with connections to railway stations, freight depots, warehouses, and so on. This company built about 60 miles of tunnels. The Chicago Tunnel Company was then formed to work in con-junction with the Warehouse Company, and they com-menced joint working in May 1912.

There are some 62 miles of tunnels at a depth of 40 ft. Through them runs railway track of 2-ft. gauge, the same as that of the London Post Office Railway. Electric locomotives are used which take current from overhead wires attached to the roof of the 7 ft. 6 in. high tunnels. The width of the tunnels, in general, is 6 ft.

There are some 3,500 freight wagons in use, most of them being 12 ft. in length and 4 ft. wide, and fitted with upright posts to which are attached timber planks to form an openwork body. Some of the bodies have a steel openwork structure. There are also metal coal wagons holding 4 tons of coal each. Wagons used for disposal of spoil from the basements of new buildings hold 3½ cu. yd. These latter are also used for ashes.

The trains are hauled by locomotives, of which some 150 are in use, and are controlled by a dispatcher at a central point. He keeps in touch with train movements by means of a complicated telephone network. All the tunnels are one way only and are lighted at inter-sections. The motormen can see by signs in the tunnels just where they are in relation to the streets above.

Much of the traffic in the tunnels consists of freight transferred between main-line railway terminals, but some goes to business concerns which have elevators to raise the trucks into their premises from special ap-proach tunnels. Warehouses despatch goods direct to railway stations through the tunnel system. Coal wagons are loaded at coal depots through overhead chutes running down to the tunnels, and the trucks then run to the premises of large users for the coal to be fed direct to the furnaces.

Most of the traffic takes its way under the busy "loop" district of Chicago, and the tunnels run under practically every street in the district from the river as far south as 16th Street. This widespread network re-lieves street congestion and also enables ashes and the spoil previously mentioned to be taken out of the area through the tunnels. The Tunnel Company has its own quay on the north bank of the river where these materials can be loaded into barges to be taken out into Lake Michigan and dumped.

At one time the tunnels carried mails, and they still contain pneumatic tubes for Press messages. The public can use the tunnel service by handing in consignments at one of the four Universal Freight Depots. These con-signments are sorted by the staff of the company and sent through the tunnels to the appropriate main-line station for onward despatch.

In 1893, the patenting of a perpetual-motion railroad was announced in the U.S.A. The patentee was a Boston physician, Hosea W. Sibley. His idea was to have two sets of tracks, one above the other, each having abrupt rises and falls but with the lowest points of the upper track being over the highest of the lower, —and so on.

The car started from an inclined plane with its trucks in the lower set of tracks. The car also had trolley wheels, and as the car ran down the slopes it came to a point where these trolley wheels engaged with the upper track. At this point the lower track fell sharply away, leaving the car running suspended from the trolley wheels and running down a gentle slope which continued long enough for the car to work up a fair speed. It then reached a point where the lower track rose to meet it and the weight was again taken on the lower wheels, which lifted the upper wheels clear of the upper track as the car ran, under its momentum, up a short slope. At a given point the upper wheels again engaged the upper track, which had also risen, and the lower track fell away again, leaving the trolley wheels to carry the car as it ran down another slope to a point where the lower wheels engaged the lower track which lifted the upper wheels off the upper track. . . and so *ad infinitum*—or at least, so the inventor claimed.

Mr. Sibley proposed to build a full-scale line round one of the World's Fair Buildings and let a car run non-stop for the duration of the Exhibition. But there must have been a hitch somewhere, for the line does not appear to have been built. This might have been called the line that ran downhill all the way. It bears a remarkable resemblance to Halford's idea in Britain, except that Halford realised that an outside power would be needed to keep his continuous downhill gradient. We have mentioned Halford's system elsewhere in the book.

Last but one we come to a railway which was unusual in its period, track, and motive power. It was the first railway in Australia, a five-mile line laid with wooden rails which connected Taranna on Norfolk Bay, the shipping station, with Deep Bay. This was in Tasmania, then called Van Diemens Land. The motive power for trucks or passenger cars was a gang of convicts who sometimes did the double journey, with its considerable gradients, twice in the day.

The deviser of this line was Charles O'Hara Booth, who took over command of the convict settlement at Port Arthur in 1833. The line was built as a link in the route by land and sea thence to Hobart, the capital. The last 1½ miles of the journey were probably the most popular with the convicts, for this was a down-hill stretch where they could climb aboard and let the truck have its head. Speeds of 40–50 m.p.h. are said to have been registered on this stretch.

Last on the list is a railway which we put forward with some reservation. All the evidence for it lies in a single print said to have been produced in 1714. There is no evidence that the date or the print are authentic, but we like to think that they are.

The print, reproduced in this book, appeared in *The Picture Magazine* in 1894. It purports to show a miniature railway constructed by order of Louis XIV of France in his park at Marly-le-Roi. A carriage ran on the rails, bearing in state members of the Royal family, who were propelled by servants pushing at the back and sides of the car. If the date of 1714 is correct, it will be seen that not only were the rails not dissimilar to those in use in recent times, but also that turntables for railway use have a long history. This almost certainly was the first pleasure railway ever built.

INDEX